# Simple
# Stories
# JESUS
# TOLD

## 13 Lessons & Songs
## for Young Children

. . . . . . . . . . . . . . . . . . . . . . . . . . . . . . . . . . .

## by Mary Rice Hopkins

Group
Loveland, Colorado

## Group resources actually work!

This Group resource helps you focus on **"The 1 Thing"™**—a life-changing relationship with Jesus Christ. "The 1 Thing" incorporates our **R.E.A.L.** approach to ministry. It reinforces a growing friendship with Jesus, encourages long-term learning, and results in life transformation, because it's:

### Relational
Learner-to-learner interaction enhances learning and builds Christian friendships.

### Experiential
What learners experience through discussion and action sticks with them up to 9 times longer than what they simply hear or read.

### Applicable
The aim of Christian education is to equip learners to be both hearers and doers of God's Word.

### Learner-based
Learners understand and retain more when the learning process takes into consideration how they learn best.

## Simple Stories Jesus Told: 13 Lessons and Songs for Young Children

Copyright © 2004 Mary Rice Hopkins

### Visit our Web site: www.grouppublishing.com

## Credits

Contributing Authors: Mary Rice Hopkins, Gwyn D. Borcherding, Nancy Wendland Feehrer, Brooke Gibson, Donna Simcoe, and Lisa Newman Wheeler
Editors: Mikal Keefer and Amy Nappa
Chief Creative Officer: Joani Schultz
Copy Editor: Ann M. Diaz
Art Director: Helen Harrison
Book Design and Production: Toolbox Creative
Cover Art Director: Bambi Eitel
Cover Designer & Photographer: Koechel Peterson & Associates
Production Manager: Peggy Naylor

**Library of Congress Cataloging-in-Publication Data**
Hopkins, Mary Rice.
    Simple stories Jesus told : 13 lessons and songs for young children /
by Mary Rice Hopkins. -- 1st American pbk. ed.
        p.  cm.
Includes bibliographical references and index.
ISBN 0-7644-2640-0 (pbk. : alk. paper)
1. Jesus Christ--Parables--Study and teaching (Preschool)  I. Title.
BT377.H67 2004
268' .432--dc22                                    2003027023

10 9 8 7 6 5 4 3 2 1     13 12 11 10 09 08 07 06 05 04
Printed in the United States of America.

### CD Credits

Executive Producer: Mary Rice Hopkins
Produced & Arranged by: Steve Williams, Denny Bouchard, Mary Rice Hopkins
Production Coordinator: Christian Michael Macey
Mixed by: Steve Williams and Denny Bouchard
Mastered by: Bernie Becker
Sequencing: Steve Williams and Denny Bouchard
Engineered by: Steve Williams, Denny Bouchard, Christian Michael Macey
Recorded at: Bernie Becker Recording, Burbank, CA
DJB Group, West Hills, CA
Backyard Studios, Montrose, CA

# Table of Contents

# Introduction

Preschoolers love music, and they especially love the music of Mary Rice Hopkins! Mary has been writing and singing songs for children for more than twenty years and has a special way of touching the hearts of kids with her tunes. Now you can use one of Mary's popular CDs as a tool for teaching your preschoolers about the parables of Jesus.

In this book you'll find a copy of Mary's *Simple Stories Jesus Told* CD. This CD focuses on the stories Jesus told to teach others important truths. Each lesson in this book centers on one of these songs and the parable that goes with it. For each parable you'll find a welcoming activity, a creative way to teach children the parable, a child-friendly craft, a tasty snack, a fun game, a meaningful prayer, and lyrics to the song along with ideas for creative movements.

You'll also find personal messages from Mary throughout *Simple Stories Jesus Told.* These messages will encourage you and give you insight into the hearts of little ones.

**God bless you as you teach them the stories Jesus taught!**

# Parable of the Lost Sheep

## PARABLE POINT God Cares for Us

### Luke 15:3-7

In this lesson you'll help your preschoolers discover that God loves and cares for them as together you explore the parable of the lost sheep.

• • • • • • • • • • • • • • • • • • • • • • • • • • • • • • • • • • • • • •

## A Message From Mary

Wow! Is there anything more important than helping children discover that God loves them? That's the point you'll make with this lesson. God loves each child in your care. And God will go to any length to reach each child.

When I wrote the song you'll sing today, I was thinking about what a poor shepherd I'd be. Give me a hundred sheep to watch and I doubt I'd notice if one came up missing. I can't tell one sheep from another.

But <u>this</u> shepherd could tell. And he was determined to find that one lost sheep and bring it back to the fold. It's easy to love a shepherd like that, isn't it?

God bless you for the hugs you give, the snacks you serve, and the songs you sing. Your kindness and smiles communicate to your children the love of the best shepherd of all—Jesus!

• • • • • • • • • • • • • • • • • • • • • • • • • • • • • • • • • • • • • •

## Supply List

- ❑ Bible
- ❑ CD player
- ❑ *Simple Stories Jesus Told* CD (track 1)
- ❑ lamb or sheep puppet or plush toy
- ❑ cotton balls
- ❑ small, empty cardboard box
- ❑ 1 plastic spoon per child

- ❑ animal crackers
- ❑ napkins
- ❑ one 4x6 index card per child
- ❑ markers or crayons
- ❑ disposable cups of water
- ❑ 100 pennies in a clear plastic jar
- ❑ clear tape

### For Extra Fun!
• • • • • • • • • • • • •

Cuddles is the perfect little lamb for this lesson. Ask about Cuddles at your favorite Christian supplier, or order him at www.grouppublishing .com.

# Welcoming Activity: Where Is the Penny?

## For Extra Fun!

It's unlikely children will find the penny without your help. If you have time, turn this into a game by telling children you know where the penny is and that if they get close to it, you'll tell them they're "warm." Help children discover where the penny is hiding!

Before children arrive, place ninety-nine pennies in a clear plastic jar. Put a lid on the jar and secure it so little hands can't reach the pennies—they're a choking hazard. Tape one shiny penny to the bottom of one of your shoes with clear tape.

After you've warmly greeted preschoolers, hold up your penny jar and ask: **Can you guess how many pennies I have in my jar?** Affirm all guesses, then say: **It's a big number. I have ninety-nine pennies in my jar, but I'm supposed to have one hundred pennies here. One of my pennies is lost. Would you help me find it? I don't want it to feel lost and alone!**

With the children, search the room. Check under chairs, on the floor, everywhere. Then call the children back together and say: **We looked everywhere, didn't we? I guess my poor penny is lost. But wait—I know somewhere we didn't look! We didn't look at the bottoms of our shoes! Maybe my penny is stuck on a shoe!**

As children check shoe bottoms, let them discover that the penny is on your shoe sole. Take the penny off, place it in the jar, and again attach the jar's lid securely. Say: **Thank you for your help! Now I have one hundred pennies again. All my pennies are safe here in my penny jar.** Ask:

- **Why do you think I care about one penny when I have ninety-nine safe in the bank?**
- **If I were a teacher with one hundred children, do you think I'd care if one child were lost?**

Let children answer and then say: **Of course I would! Why do you think it would matter to me so much if you were lost?** Allow time for response.

**Today I'm going to tell you a parable—a story that Jesus told to help people understand what God is like. God is like a shepherd who takes care of his sheep.**

**Good shepherds always know how many sheep they have. They know when one of their little sheep gets lost or hurt. And good shepherds take care of their sheep.**

**I'd like to tell you the story Jesus told—and I've brought a helper: Shelly Sheepshanks.** Bring out the lamb puppet or plush toy. **Shelly is a lamb. Tell Shelly "hello."** Allow time for children to respond, and have Shelly enthusiastically wave, nod her head, or respond to the children in another way as you say in a slightly affected voice, **"Hi, kids! Good to see you! Let's hear that story about shepherds and sheep!"**

# Parable Discovery:
## Parable of the Lost Sheep

Sit in a chair and gather children in front of you. Set your puppet or stuffed lamb on your lap. Show children your open Bible. Say: **Jesus first told this story, and it's in our Bibles in the book of Luke.**

Use the following script to tell the parable.

**Teacher:** This story is about shepherds and sheep. How many of you have ever seen a real sheep? Raise your hands.

**Shelly:** Hey—*I'm* a real sheep!

**Teacher:** You're a real *pretend* sheep. I mean a *real* sheep that has a thick, pretty coat.

**Shelly:** *I* have a thick, pretty coat!

**Teacher:** I mean a sheep that has a cute little tail that wags.

**Shelly:** *I* have a cute little tail that wags!

**Teacher:** I mean a sheep that eats grass for lunch.

**Shelly:** *(Pausing)* You're right: I'm *not* a real sheep. I like *pizza* for lunch!

**Teacher:** This little sheep lived with ninety-nine friends. And there was one shepherd who took care of all of them.

**Shelly:** Did the shepherd tuck them in at night?

**Teacher:** The shepherd did even more than that. He helped them find food to eat and water to drink. He kept them from getting lost. He took care of them if scary, wild animals got too close. He was a good friend to all the sheep.

**Shelly:** What a nice guy!

**Teacher:** That's right. One time, when it was late at night and the shepherd was putting his sheep to sleep, he found that one little lamb was missing. So you know what he did?

**Shelly:** He said, "Bye-bye, little lost lamb! I'm staying here with the other ninety-nine sheep who aren't out sheep-walking."

**Teacher:** No! He said, "I can't sleep a wink until I find my sheep." So he got up and looked for his sheep. Children, help let's help the shepherd look. He looked high… *(Shield your eyes and look up.)* He looked low… *(Shield your eyes and look down.)* He looked far… *(Shield your eyes and look out into the distance.)* And he looked near… *(Look at the ground.)* And finally he found his little lost sheep.

**Shelly:** Did he get angry at the sheep?

**Teacher:** Not at all. He said, "I've found my sheep! I'm so happy!" He put the sheep on his shoulders and carried the sheep all the way home. He called his friends and neighbors and said, "Let's have a party! I found my lost sheep!"

**Shelly:** What a great shepherd! But I have a question.

**Teacher:** What's that?

**Shelly:** Why did Jesus tell that story? To remind us sheep not to get lost?

**Teacher:** It's always good to not run away and get lost. But that's not why Jesus told us the story. Jesus wanted us to know that he's like the shepherd. Do any of you children remember what shepherds do for their sheep? *(Affirm answers.)* Good shepherds take care of their sheep. And **God takes care of us!** Turn to a friend and tell your friend one way God takes care of you. *(Pause as children talk together.)* Good job! It's time to say goodbye to our friend, Shelly Sheepshanks. Say "goodbye," kids!

**PARABLE POINT**

Place your sheep puppet or stuffed animal where it's not visible to the children and continue.

# Sing and Celebrate: "Farmer and the Sheep" (track 1)

• • • • • • • • • • • • • • • • • • • • • • • • • • • • • • • • • • •

This fun song is perfect for waking up and looking surprised! As you lead this song, feel free to create motions to go along with the words. Lead children in these actions during the chorus:

- When the shepherd is supposed to be asleep, have children pretend to lay their heads on their hands, then wake up.
- When the lyrics say the shepherd couldn't sleep, have children wag their fingers back and forth.

And as always, let children move to the music. It's easier if children are standing, so go through the song while they're on their feet.

## "Farmer and the Sheep"

The farmer is looking for his sheep.

He can't find him, and he can't sleep.

He looks high, he looks low,

And he looks to the mountains

And the rivers below.

*(Chorus)*

Oh, no! He can't sleep

Until he finds his little, lost sheep.

Oh, no! He can't sleep

Until he finds his sheep.

The sheep could be the only one.

Through the briars, through the meadows,

He calls him to come.

He looks up, he looks down.

And he keeps on looking until he is found.

*(Repeat chorus.)*

He can't sleep a wink.

No, he can't eat.

'Cause he missed his little lost sheep.

*(Repeat.)*

When he comes back to the fold,

The farmer celebrates

With the young and old.

He thanks God, for he's found.

And he has a big party and invites the town.

*(Last chorus)*

Oh, yeah, now he can sleep.

But he wants to stay awake

And party with the sheep.

Oh, yeah, now he can sleep.

But he wants to party with the sheep.

*(Repeat.)*

Celebrating with the sheep,

He wants to party with the sheep.

## "God Cares for Animals" Snack

Serve animal crackers and glasses of cool water. Encourage children to look for animal crackers that might be sheep and to talk about how God takes care of sheep and other animals. Ask children who have family pets what they do to care for their pets.

Use this casual discussion time to enter into your kids' lives, finding out what's important to them this week. You may not be able to spend a lot of time talking about sheep and our Good Shepherd, but by being a trusted, listening adult, you are helping shepherd the young sheep in your class!

## Allergy Alert

Be aware that some children have food allergies that can be dangerous. Know your children, and consult with parents about allergies your kids may have. Also be sure to read food labels carefully as hidden ingredients can cause allergy problems.

**PARABLE POINT**

## "I Care" Card Craft

Give each child a 4x6 index card. Explain what you're asking children to do *before* you distribute markers.

Say: **God cares for us just like a good shepherd cares for his sheep. We can care for others, too.**

**Today let's think about how we can care for our moms or dads. Usually our parents take care of us, but today we're going to take care of them!**

**Maybe we can show we care by helping set the table, or by picking up our toys, or by giving our moms or dads a big hug. On your card draw a picture of yourself doing something that shows you caring for your mom or dad. We'll take our cards home and give them to our moms or dads.**

Encourage children to talk with you or other adults as they draw. Ask about what they're drawing, compliment their cards, and make sure you put a name on each card so you can send it home with the correct child at the end of class.

## Sheep Roundup Game

Give each child a plastic spoon. Place an empty box near the center of the room. Scatter white cotton balls all around the room.

Ask children to pick up the cotton balls with their spoons and drop the cotton balls in the box.

Say: **You'll have to move fast—we can only herd our sheep back safely to the "sheep pen" as long as the music is playing.** Play "Farmer and the Sheep" (track 1) as you and the children round up your sheep.

Consider playing the song several times to make sure all the sheep get home to the sheep pen safely. Thank your children for being good shepherds who care for their sheep—just like **God cares for us!**

**PARABLE POINT**

# Together Prayer: Thank You, Lord

Say: **We have a good shepherd who cares for us. It's God! Let's think of ways God takes care of us, such as making sure we have food. Or he gives us parents who love us. Or he lets us come to church and be with friends.**

**Now let's take turns thanking God for what he does. I might say, "Thank you, God, for letting me be with my friends here today. I love these kids!"**

**Let's close our eyes, fold our hands, and take turns thanking God for something.**

Be clear about your expectations. Don't force any child to pray—but do be clear that it's OK to pray, and that we should thank God for being a good shepherd and caring for us. Help children know when to pray by softly inviting them to pray by name, taking turns as you go around the circle.

## Teacher Tip

Gather your children in a circle, and encourage them to bow their heads and fold their hands— that posture will help them focus. Form more than one circle if you have other leaders in your room who can lead prayer circles too.

# Parable of the Prodigal Son

**PARABLE POINT** God Loves You
Luke 15:11-24

Comfort. Safety. Love. For many people, these are the joys of coming home. In the parable of the prodigal son, preschoolers will discover that God loves them and welcomes them into his arms.

• • • • • • • • • • • • • • • • • • • • • • • • • • • • • • • • • • • • • • • • •

## A Message From Mary

The parable of the prodigal son...what a great story!

As I was writing the song "Come on Home," I reflected on how this parable shares the heart of the Gospel. The story lets me know just how amazing God's love is. Not only does God love us, but he also keeps loving us and offering us forgiveness. God welcomes us home with open arms and then celebrates our arrival...even when we've messed up and gone our own direction.

That's the kind of father you're helping your children get to know—a dad who won't be mad when they come home.

Thanks for all you do to communicate this special love to the children in your care.

• • • • • • • • • • • • • • • • • • • • • • • • • • • • • • • • • • • • • • • • •

## Supply List

❑ CD player

❑ *Simple Stories Jesus Told* CD (track 2)

❑ Bible

❑ large box with "lost and found" items such as hats, mittens, and sweaters

❑ small cups of fruit ring cereal

❑ disposable cups of water

❑ 8½x11 sheets of light- or bright-colored construction paper

❑ safety scissors

❑ stapler

❑ markers or crayons

❑ 2 shoe boxes

❑ robe

❑ hat

❑ green construction paper "money"

❑ small bag

❑ masking tape

# Welcoming Activity: Lost and Found

Before children arrive, fill a box with "lost and found" items such as a hat, one mitten, a sweater, a pencil, and so on.

Have the children sit in a circle on the floor. Greet the children, and let them know you are happy they've come. Then say: **I have a special box I want to show you. It's called a "Lost and Found" box. Have you ever heard of a "Lost and Found" box?** Let the children guess about its use.

**If you lose something at church or school or even at the mall, sometimes those lost things end up in a "Lost and Found" box. I'm going to hand each of you something from this box. I want you to hold it in your lap until it's your turn. When it's your turn, I want you to make up a little story about how this thing might have gotten lost.**

Begin by making up a short story about an item. Then go around the circle, and let each child tell about his or her "lost" item. After each turn, have the child put the item back in the box.

When the stories are finished, ask for a volunteer. Have the child stand next to the box. Ask: **What if a child gets lost? Does the child get put in a box?** Let the children respond. Then say: **No! Of course not! Have you ever been lost? What happened? What did it feel like?** Give the children a few minutes for their stories.

**Today I'm going to tell you about a boy who was lost—but he was lost in a different way. Jesus told this story to show how much  God loves you.**

## For Extra Fun!

This brings a smile every time! Instead of asking for a child to volunteer to be the "lost" child, use a cardboard box that is large enough for an older child to hide in. Hand out one "lost and found" item from the box to each child, but have the older child hide inside until the end. Then pretend to lift up the child from the box, and continue with the lesson.

**PARABLE POINT**

# Parable Discovery:
## Parable of the Prodigal Son

Sit in a chair, and have the children sit on the floor facing you. Open your Bible to Luke 15:11-24. Show the children your open Bible, and say: **Jesus told this story to a group of people who were gathered around him. He told it to help the people understand that God loves them, and  God loves you, too! We're going to call this a "pop-up parable," and I'm going to need your help to tell the story.**

Ask for volunteers to be the Son and the Father. The rest of the children can be the Chorus. Say: **When I point to the Son or the Father or the Chorus, I want you to pop up from your seat, say the words that I tell you, then sit back down.**

**PARABLE POINT**

**Are you ready to practice?** Practice for a couple minutes using the lines below:

**Father:** I love you, son!

**Son:** I want to leave our home!

**Chorus:** Bad choice, son!

When you are sure they understand, use the following script to tell the parable.

**Teacher:** There was a man...*(Point to the Father.)*

**Father:** *(Pops up.)* I love you, son!

**Teacher:** ...who had two sons. The younger son went to his father one day and said...*(Point to the Son.)*

**Son:** *(Pops up.)* I want to leave our home!

**Chorus:** *(Pops up.)* Bad choice, son!

**Teacher:** The father...*(Point to the Father.)*

**Father:** *(Pops up.)* I love you, son!

**Teacher:** ...was sad to let his son go. But he divided his money and gave it to each of his sons. Then he let his younger son go. *(Point to the Son and then the Chorus and then the Father.)*

**Son:** *(Pops up.)* I want to leave our home!

**Chorus:** *(Pops up.)* Bad choice, son!

**Father:** *(Pops up.)* I love you, son!

**Teacher:** And so the son...*(Point to the Son.)*

**Son:** *(Pops up.)* I want to leave our home!

**Teacher:** ...got together all he had, and left for a far-off country. While he was there, he wasted all his money in wild living. *(Point to the Chorus.)*

**Chorus:** *(Pops up.)* Bad choice, son!

**Teacher:** After he had spent everything, there was a bad time called a famine in that country. No one had anything to eat! The son began to be in need. So he went and got a job feeding pigs. He was so hungry that he wanted to eat the pigs' food!

**Chorus:** *(Pops up.)* Bad choice, son!

**Teacher:** But no one gave him anything. Finally, he got smart. *(Point to the Chorus. Ask them to say, "Good choice, son!")*

**Chorus:** *(Pops up.)* Good choice, son!

**Teacher:** The son thought about it for a while. "My father's servants have lots of food, and here I am starving! I'll go back to my father and say, 'I've sinned against God and you. I'm too bad to be called your son.' Then I'll ask to be one of his servants." *(Point to the Son. Ask him to say, "I want to come on home!")*

**Son:** *(Pops up.)* I want to come on home!

**Chorus:** *(Pops up.)* Good choice, son!

**Teacher:** But while the son was still a long way off, his father saw him and was filled with love for him. He ran to his son, threw his arms around him, and kissed him! *(Point to the Father.)*

**Father:** *(Pops up.)* I love you, son!

**Teacher:** The son said to his father, "I have sinned against God and against you. I shouldn't even be called your son!" But the father called to his servants, "Quick! Bring the best robe and put it on him. Put a ring on his finger and sandals on his feet. Let's have a party and celebrate! For this son of mine was lost and now is found!" *(Point to the Son and then the Chorus and then the Father.)*

**Son:** *(Pops up.)* I want to come on home!

**Chorus:** *(Pops up.)* Good choice, son!

**Father:** *(Pops up.)* I love you, son!

Say: **Great job! Give yourselves a clap! Jesus used this story to teach us that  God loves you! The father in the story is like our heavenly Father, God. The son in the story is like you and me. Sometimes we make bad choices, but God still loves us and welcomes us to him with open arms! We can always come home to God.**

**PARABLE POINT**

# Sing and Celebrate:
## "Come On Home" (track 2)

The parable of the prodigal son includes lots of travel! "Travel" around your room as you march to the beat of this catchy song!

Clear a path around the outside edge of your room for the children to march around as you sing this song together. Stop and face the center of the room during the chorus and do some of these motions if you like. Each time you hear these lines in the song, use these motions:

- "Come on home!" *(Move your hand and arm from your side up and over your head like a gathering motion.)*
- "Your father will be waiting." *(Stop and tap your foot.)*
- "Your dad won't be mad." *(Make a mad face and shake your finger as if you were scolding.)*
- "In fact, he'll be glad." *(Smile and open your arms like a hug.)*
- "When you come home." *(Stretch both arms out, and move your hands in a gathering motion.)*

# "Come On Home"

I've got two sons,

As different as can be.

Both of them are special

In our family.

One of them, he works so hard

And helps us in our home.

The other was dissatisfied

And said, "I want to roam.

I want to roam."

Well, I was sad when he said, "Dad,

I just want my money."

So he took his inheritance

And went where it was sunny.

Then he spent all that he had;

He squandered every dime.

He was so pitiful, eating with the swine,

The pigs and swine.

*(Chorus)*

So come on home.

Your father will be waiting.

Come on home.

Oh, we're anticipating.

Come on home.

Turn around and change your ways.

'Cause your dad won't be mad.

In fact, he'll be glad.

Your dad won't be mad
When you come home.

Then he saw his foolish ways
And returned to the farm.
My heart leapt for joy,
And I opened up the barn.
Then we ate the fatted cow
With everyone around.
My son had been lost,
But now he's been found.
He's been found.

Then I placed a golden ring
Upon his hand.
We danced and sang all night
And played with the band.
My son said, "I love you, Dad.
I'll never leave again.
Your forgiveness has brought me home.
You are my friend, my best friend."

*(Repeat chorus.)*

# Ring Wing-Ding!

Pair up the children. Explain that in the story of the prodigal son, the father was so happy to see his son come home that he gave his son fancy clothes and a fancy ring for his finger.

Say: **Let's have a party—a "Ring Wing-Ding"—to celebrate that God loves you!** Serve colorful fruit ring cereal and cups of water.

This snack will remind the children of the fancy ring that the father gave his son. Tell them that God is our Father in heaven and that he gives us gifts too. They are called blessings. Encourage the children to talk to their partners about these three questions as they munch on their snacks:

- **What do you like about your home?**
- **How do you know God loves you?**
- **What can you do to show God you love him?**

 ## Allergy Alert

Be aware that some children have food allergies that can be dangerous. Know your children, and consult with parents about allergies your kids may have. Also be sure to read food labels carefully as hidden ingredients can cause allergy problems.

# Heart-Filled Homes

Before class, take two differently colored sheets of construction paper, and stack the darker color on top of the lighter color. On each of the long sides, staple the paper twice, once near the center and once about two inches down, as shown in the diagram. You should have four staples all together—two on each side. Make one set of papers for each child.

Give each child one set of stapled papers and a pair of scissors. Have each child cut the paper as you show an example. First, cut the top two corners off to form a "roof" shape. Next, carefully cut the top paper sheet from the bottom, up about half way, then across in a T. Fold the paper open on each side to create doors.

Let each child decorate his or her "house" with markers and crayons. Encourage children to each draw a welcoming parent inside the doors of their homes. As children work, go around and write, "God Loves You!" on the inside of each home.

**PARABLE POINT**

Say: **These houses can remind you of the boy who came home to his father, and that God is always welcoming you because** God loves you!

# "The Prodigal Son" Obstacle Course

Set up a mini obstacle course in your room to act out the story of the prodigal son. You'll need four stations.

- At station 1, place a hat, a bag, and a pile of money (cut green construction paper) in a shoe box.
- At station 2, place an empty shoe box to hold the money.
- At station 3, make a square of masking tape on the floor for a pigpen.
- At station 4, place a robe on a chair to represent "home."

Let each child go through the obstacle course. At station 1, the child should stuff the play money in the bag and put on the hat. At station 2, the child should dump the money into the shoe box. At station 3, the child should get on all fours inside the pigpen square and oink a few times. At station 4, the child should put on the robe and sit in the chair. Have a helper return the items to their proper stations as children finish with them so they'll be there for the next child moving through the game.

As you let each child try the obstacle course, listen to the song "Come On Home" (track 2). You may also want to have the children walk on their knees to each station, so they won't be tempted to run in the classroom.

# Responsive Prayer: Lost and Found

Say: God loves you! Just like the father in our story today, we have a Father in heaven who loves us no matter what! Just like the son in the story, sometimes we disobey God, and when we do we may feel "lost." I'm going to say a prayer. In the first part of the prayer, I'm going to list some times when we might feel lost or far away from God. After each thing I list, I want you to say: "I'm lost and far from home."

Then I'll list some things that make us feel close to God. When I do, I want you to say: "I'm found in God's love." I'll let you know what to say.

Let's close our eyes and fold our hands.

Dear God,

When I disobey my parents…I'm lost and far from home.

When I am mean to my friends…I'm lost and far from home.

When I refuse to share…I'm lost and far from home.

When I only want my way…I'm lost and far from home.

I know that you love me no matter what. Your love helps me to do what's right.

When I obey my parents…I'm found in God's love!

When I am kind to my friends…I'm found in God's love!

When I share what I have…I'm found in God's love!

When I let others have their way…I'm found in God's love!

Help me to always remember how much you love me. In Jesus' name, amen.

# Parable of the Good Samaritan

## PARABLE POINT We Can Be Helpers

Luke 10:25-37

Young children often hear about the things they *can't* do. But every child can be a helper. In this lesson you'll help your preschoolers discover they can help others as you explore the parable of the good Samaritan.

• • • • • • • • • • • • • • • • • • • • • • • • • • • • • • • • • • • • • • • • •

## A Message From Mary

The little ones in your care are developing the attitudes they will carry for the rest of their lives. You can lead them to be the kind of people that make the world a better place by helping others.

It doesn't always come naturally! More often than not, it's much easier to walk away than to help someone in need. Yet one of the greatest stories in the Bible is the story of the good Samaritan. It shows us who the true neighbor is and who really helped the person who was lying there in the road.

I think the most important part of this song, "Who Is Your Neighbor?" is the question, "Who will be Jesus to them?" Through this simple story and song, we can share God's love and compassion. You, as teachers, have a tremendous opportunity to be Jesus to your children and teach them to be Jesus to others. Thank you for all you do.

• • • • • • • • • • • • • • • • • • • • • • • • • • • • • • • • • • • • • • • • •

## Supply List

- ❏ CD player
- ❏ *Simple Stories Jesus Told* CD (track 3)
- ❏ Bible
- ❏ crayons
- ❏ blanket
- ❏ 16-ounce plastic foam cups

- ❏ chenille wires
- ❏ plastic ware
- ❏ napkins
- ❏ crackers
- ❏ individually wrapped cheese slices
- ❏ disposable cups of water

# Welcoming Activity: Handy Helpers

Greet children warmly as they arrive, then continue to busy yourself in the room—rearranging supplies and moving chairs as if you're still preparing for class. Invite children by name to help you in these various tasks. Make sure each child is invited to be a helper for at least one task. For example, spill a container of markers, then call several children by name and say: **Oh, no! What a mess! Would you please be helpers and pick these up for me?** Ask several other children to help rearrange chairs in the room. Have others spread a blanket on the floor for use in the "Parable Discovery" activity. As children help, affirm their efforts with a warm smile and a pat on the back or a hug.

When everyone has had an opportunity to help, gather the class to sit on the blanket, and thank the children. Say: **Thank you so much for being helpers! I needed your help to be prepared for class. I really appreciate your help!** Ask:

- **How does it feel to be a helper?**
- **Who are people that need your help?**
- **What are ways you help at home?**

Say: **Moms, dads, and other people are thankful for our help, and it feels great to help them. One time Jesus told a story about someone who needed help. I would like to tell you that story, but I'll need your help to do it. Would you help me again? When I turn my thumbs down, you do the same and say, "Oh, no!" When I hold my thumbs up, you do the same and shout, "Yippee!"**

Practice the thumbs up and thumbs down responses with kids several times.

## Teacher Tip

Consider the number of children in your class, and plan ahead for other tasks with which children can help. Preschoolers can wipe off tables, set out snack supplies, dust countertops, sweep floors, or straighten bookshelves. Keep kids busy helping with one task or another as time allows.

# Parable Discovery:
# Parable of the Good Samaritan

Show children your open Bible. Say: **Jesus first told this story, and it's in our Bibles in the book of Luke.** As you tell the parable, lead children to use the thumbs up (Yippee!) and thumbs down (Oh, no!) signs.

Use the following script to tell the parable.

**A man was traveling from Jerusalem to a town called Jericho. It was a long walk, and the road went down between high rocky areas. The road**

seemed empty. No one else was in sight, but the man wasn't alone. Someone was watching him. Mean men were hiding behind the rocks. They surprised the man, beat him up, took his money and his clothes, and left him there. Give the thumbs down sign and lead children in saying, "Oh, no!"

The man lay there too hurt to get up. He was too hurt to even call for help. Soon, another traveler came along the road. The hurt man thought, "Oh good, here comes a man. Perhaps he will help me!" Give the thumbs up sign and lead children in saying, "Yippee!"

But when the traveler saw the hurt man, he moved over to the other side of the road, away from the hurt man. Perhaps he was scared the robbers might hurt him, too! Maybe there were more bad men hiding in the rocks. The hurt man watched the traveler hurry away. Give the thumbs down sign and lead children in saying, "Oh, no!"

Some time later he heard more footsteps. Another traveler was coming! The hurt man thought, "Surely this person will help me!" Give the thumbs up sign and lead children in saying, "Yippee!"

But just like the first traveler, this man moved to the other side of the road, away from the hurt man. Perhaps he was in a hurry and thought he didn't have time to help. Stopping to help would take a while, and then he'd be late for work. The hurt man watched sadly as the traveler walked by. Give the thumbs down sign and lead children in saying, "Oh, no!"

A long time passed and the hurt man felt lonely and scared. Then, he heard the *clip-clop* of a donkey's hooves. Someone else was coming. Give the thumbs up sign and lead children in saying, "Yippee!"

This time the hurt man thought, "No one will help me. This person probably won't stop. He'll ride his donkey right past me." Give the thumbs down sign and lead children in saying, "Oh, no!"

But guess what? This man did not ride past! He stopped! Give the thumbs up sign and lead children in saying, "Yippee!" He helped! Repeat the thumbs up sign. He cleaned and bandaged the man's hurt places. Thumbs up. He gave him a drink. Thumbs up. Then he put the hurt man on his donkey and took him into town. Thumbs up. He took the hurt man to a house and took care of him all night long. The next day when the helper had to leave, he gave money to the owner of the house and asked him to take care of the hurt man until he was better. Thumbs up.

**Let's cheer and praise God for the man who was a helper!** Lead children to clap and shout, praising God.

**Let's remember the important things about Jesus' story. The hurt man was in trouble. Two men came, but didn't help. Sometimes people are afraid to help. Some think they are too busy. Finally someone came who was willing to help. Helping was the kind and loving thing to do. Jesus told this story to remind us that**  **we can be helpers. Turn to a friend, and tell about a time when you were loving and kind and helped someone else.** Allow time for children to share.

**PARABLE POINT**

When you have finished the story and are ready to begin the "Sing and Celebrate" activity, ask children to help by folding the blanket and putting it away.

## Sing and Celebrate:
## "Who Is Your Neighbor?" (track 3)

This gentle song will help children begin to think of others they can help. As you lead this song, gather children in a circle, holding hands and swaying to the music during the verses. Use these actions when you hear the following lines during the chorus:

- "Who is your neighbor?" *(Point slowly around the circle at others standing with you.)*
- "Who will be Jesus to him?" *(Have children put their arms around the shoulders of the children on either side of them.)*

## "Who Is Your Neighbor?"

One day a man was traveling down a dusty road.
Somebody saw him carrying a heavy load.
But there were three robbers; they took everything.
They left him lying there, beaten, in pain.
After a while another man came along.

Dressed in royalty, he was whistling a song.
He didn't stop or have pity on him.
He left him lying there alone again.

*(Chorus)*

Who is your neighbor?
Who is your friend?

Who is your neighbor?

Who will be Jesus to him?

Jesus to him?

The sun comes and goes; he's still lying there.

Other people pass, and they just stare.

A judge and a priest and a Pharisee

Passing him by, but they don't want to see.

But then someone reaches out to him.

He's from another country and another skin.

He says, "I'll help you; I don't have much,"

Sharing his home and a gentle touch.

*(Repeat chorus twice.)*

Oh, the Good Samaritan.

## "Helping Each Other" Snack

Let children help prepare this snack and serve it to their friends. Have children wash their hands, and provide a clean surface for them to work on.

Help children form pairs. Give each child a slice of cheese, a plastic knife, a napkin, and several crackers. Let kids unwrap the cheese, use their knives to cut the cheese into shapes, and stack the cheese pieces on crackers. When the snacks are prepared, have kids offer them to their partners. While children are working, pour a cup of cool water for each one.

Preschoolers experience a strong sense of accomplishment and mastery when they help others. Talk about the joy of helping, and ask children about other times that they have been helpers. Encourage kids to help with cleanup as well. Model gratitude, thanking children for their help.

 **Allergy Alert**

Be aware that some children have food allergies that can be dangerous. Know your children, and consult with parents about allergies your kids may have. Also be sure to read food labels carefully as hidden ingredients can cause allergy problems.

## "Helper's Silverware Caddy" Craft

Give each child a 16-ounce plastic foam cup; a chenille wire; a napkin; and a plastic spoon, fork, and knife. Write each child's name on a cup so children can take them home after class. Provide crayons for children to use to decorate the outside of their cups. Help each child poke the ends of the chenille stem through opposite sides of the cup's rim and twist to form a carrying handle.

Show kids how to lay the spoon, fork, and knife together on one corner of the napkin, then roll it up. Place the plasticware setting inside the cup.

Say: **We can be helpers like the traveler who helped the hurt man. People need different kinds of help. Sometimes our moms and dads need help. One way we can help them is by setting the table before mealtimes. The set in your cup is for playing, but you can use your carrier to take real silverware to the table and then lay it beside each person's plate.**

Give children time to play with their carriers and plastic ware, pretending to set and clear a table. Ask for helpers to put away the crayons. Talk with children about other ways they can be helpers in their homes.

# "Hop and Help" Game

● ● ● ● ● ● ● ● ● ● ● ● ● ● ● ● ● ● ● ● ● ● ● ● ● ● ● ● ● ● ● ●

Designate one end of your room as the starting line and the other end of the room as the finish line. Have several children at a time try to hop from one end to the other. Hopping on one foot is often difficult for preschoolers—do not force anyone to try to the point of frustration, but give each one a chance to try and experience the difficulty.

Say: **Some things are hard to do by ourselves, but  we can be helpers for each other!** Have children form pairs. One child in each pair should hop, while the helper holds both of the hopping child's hands to support and steady the friend. Lead children to discover how good it feels to receive help when we need it and to realize that their help is valuable to others.

**It's important that people who need help receive it. The man on the road couldn't help himself because he was hurt so badly. You need help when you're learning to hop. Moms and dads need help when they are busy. Since  we can be helpers, God can use us to make things easier for others. We show his love when we help others.**

**PARABLE POINT**

**PARABLE POINT**

# Together Prayer: Helping Actions Prayer

Gather children together in a group. Remind them of the various ways they have helped today, such as picking up crayons, moving chairs, preparing and cleaning up snacks, and encouraging others. Encourage children to look for other ways they can help at home. As you pray this prayer together, tell children to act out whatever form of helping you describe.

Pray: **Dear God, thank you that we can be helpers. We can help by setting the table.** Pause, allowing kids time to do actions. **We can help by picking up toys.** Pause. **We can help by being a friend.** Pause. **Help us look for ways to help others and show them your love. Amen.**

# Parable of the Lost Coin

## PARABLE POINT God Wants to Be Your Friend

### Luke 15:8-10

In this lesson you'll help your preschoolers discover that God wants to be friends with each one of us as together you explore the parable of the lost coin.

## A Message From Mary

The lost coin, the lost sheep, the lost son...I really like these themes because if anyone is "directionally challenged," it's Mary Rice Hopkins. In fact, I am always misplacing things and getting lost on the way to a concert. I even told my husband, "This song is for you."

Seriously though, aren't you glad that in God's kingdom we are never lost and he always knows where we are? In fact, he searches us out, just like the lost coin. But even better yet, when he finds us he not only rejoices, he throws a party with the angels in heaven!!! Now that's something worth celebrating. I hope as you tell the story of the lost coin being found, you will see the significance in each little life you are blessing. Thanks for the hugs you give, the snacks you serve, and most of all for the little ones you bring home!

## Supply List

- ❑ CD player
- ❑ *Simple Stories Jesus Told* CD (track 4)
- ❑ Bible
- ❑ small paper plates and cups
- ❑ disposable cups of water
- ❑ package of 10 markers
- ❑ broom

- ❑ flashlight
- ❑ toy phone
- ❑ aluminum foil
- ❑ unsharpened pencils
- ❑ napkins
- ❑ honeycomb-shaped cereal

# Welcoming Activity: Count to Ten

Before children arrive, remove a red marker from the package of ten, and hide it in the room. Be sure other markers that may be in the room are out of sight. Set out ten cups, ten paper plates, and the box of markers.

As children arrive greet them warmly, and then gather them together. Say: **I like to collect things in groups of ten. Let's see if all of my things are here. Will you help me count?** Count the cups, then the plates, encouraging children to count with you. Ask: **What else can you use to count to ten?** Affirm answers, then say: **I have ten fingers and ten toes. Turn to a neighbor, and let's count fingers.** Allow pairs to take turns counting each other's fingers as you lead the counting for the group. **Now let's see if all ten of my markers are here.** Count with the children, and notice the missing item. **Oh, no! I'm missing the red one! That's disappointing! I need every one for my collection.** Ask:

- **Have you ever lost something special to you? How did you feel?**
- **What did you do to find it?**

Listen to answers, then say: **Let's look around and see if we can find my missing marker.** Help children search the room, and give hints if necessary to help children find the red marker.

When it is found, say: **Thank you for helping me find my missing marker. It is nice to have the whole set. If we hadn't found it, I could probably use a different red marker. But suppose instead of a missing _marker_, someone had a missing _friend?_ That would be very sad! God made people special. Each person is different from all the others. God loves each person and doesn't want any friends missing from his family. He doesn't want just ten friends— he wants everyone! God made _you_ special. There's no one else like you. That's why God wants to be _your_ friend.**

## Teacher Tip

Young preschoolers are just beginning to develop counting skills. Even when they recite numbers in correct order, they may not make the one-to-one correspondence of true counting. Your modeling will help them grow in this skill, but don't insist on accuracy. As children participate in these activities, allow children to count at their own developmental level. As they count foil coins or cereal pieces, you'll see a wide variation in ability. Don't worry about correcting mistakes, but affirm each one's effort.

# Parable Discovery:
# Parable of the Lost Coin

Before class, make ten coins as described in the coin craft later in this lesson. Draw a dollar sign on each one. Hide one coin somewhere in the room where it is out of sight. Stack the other nine, and gather the flashlight, broom, and toy telephone in preparation for telling the story. Sit in a chair and gather children in front of you. As you tell the story, invite individual children to participate in acting out the story as described. Show children your open Bible. Say: **Jesus first told this story, and it's in our Bibles in the book of Luke.**

Use the following script to tell the parable.

Invite one child to stand and hold the coins. Say: **Once there was a woman who had ten coins. This money was all she had to live on. The coins were very important to her. She liked to count her coins to make sure they were all there. Let's help her count them.** Invite children to help count the coins out loud. **Oh, no! There are only nine. One is missing! What should she do?** Wait for responses, then say: **Yes, she started looking for the missing coin. She turned on the light so she could see better.** Invite another child to turn on the flashlight and shine it around the room. **Then she got a broom and started sweeping in case it had fallen on the floor.** Invite another child to use the broom to sweep. **She looked everywhere!**

One at a time, invite other children to look for the coin. Ask remaining children to offer suggestions as to where the seeker should look or to take a turn with the flashlight or broom. If the coin is not found, have the seeker return and sit with the group, and allow another child to look in another spot suggested by the group. If children are unable to find the coin after several turns, suggest the next seeker look where you know the coin is hidden. Say: **She looked and looked and finally found the coin! Now she had all ten! Let's help her count them.** Count the coins aloud with the children. **She was so happy, she called her friends.** Give a child the toy phone, and have the child pretend to call friends. **She said, "I am so excited! One of my coins was lost, but now I've found it! Come over and let's have a party to celebrate!" All her friends came to celebrate. They all cheered and shouted, "Hooray!"** Have all the children stand up, jump, and shout. Then thank the actors, and gather the children again on the floor and discuss the following questions:

• **How do you think the woman felt when her coin was lost?**

• **How do you think the woman felt when she found her coin?**

• **If you found something that had been lost, whom would you call to share the good news?**

Say: **When something wonderful happens, we want to tell our friends. Our**

**PARABLE POINT**  friends are happy when good things happen to us. Friends help us when we are sad or in trouble.  God wants to be your friend. He wants to bring good things into your life, like his love and forgiveness. He wants to help you when you are sad or in trouble. Whatever happens, good or bad,  God wants to be your friend.

# Sing and Celebrate:
## "Oh Honey" (track 4)

This song has lots of wiggle-giggle potential! Energize children with these actions during the chorus:

- When the lyrics talk about looking for the coin, have children shield their eyes and look around the room.
- When the lyrics talk about kissing when the coin is found, have children blow a kiss to a friend.
- During the line about angels rejoicing, have kids wiggle their hands in the air and turn in a circle.

Encourage children to interact freely with the music and with each other. An atmosphere of joy will reinforce God's great love for children and his desire to be their friend.

## "Oh Honey"

Up in the attic, in every room,

Down in the basement with my broom.

I've searched everywhere from night till noon.

Oh, where did my little, bitty coin go?

Where did my little, bitty coin go?

*(Chorus)*

Oh, honey, I can't find my money.

I'm sweeping and cleaning and feeling kind of blue.

Oh, honey, I can't find my money.

But when I find it, I'm gonna kiss you.

The angels will rejoice too.

*(Repeat chorus.)*

Oh, my dear, look at this mess.

I've looked everywhere from east to west.

Until I find it, I won't rest.

Oh, where did my little, bitty coin go?

Oh, where did my little, bitty coin go?

*(Repeat chorus.)*

In every cranny, place, and nook,

Even in Granny's favorite book,

With my dust mop, I will look.

Where did my little, bitty coin go?

Where did my little, bitty coin go?

Jump for joy—it's been found!—

With every girl and boy in town.

When one is lost and turns around,

Rejoice with them in heaven.

Rejoice with them in heaven.

*(Last chorus)*

Oh, honey, now I've found my money.

Now I'm not feeling so blue.

Oh, honey, I've found my money.

Now I've found it, I'm gonna kiss you.

The angels are rejoicing too.

Rejoicing too. Rejoicing too. Rejoicing too.

## "Count Your Coins" Snack

Serve honeycomb-shaped cereal pieces and cups of cool water. Help children form pairs, then have each one count ten cereal pieces onto a napkin and offer it to their friend. Help children thank each other, and then enjoy the snack together. Show them how to replay the parable by hiding one piece under the napkin and counting the remaining pieces.

As children enjoy the snack, talk about friendship. Ask:

- **How can you tell someone is your friend?**
- **What does a friend do?**
- **Who are some of your friends?**

Say: **A friend cares about what happens to us. A friend will help us when we need help.**  **God wants to be your friend. He loves and cares for you. He forgives you when you do something wrong. He will always help you. God is the best friend we can have!**

**PARABLE POINT**

 ## Allergy Alert

Be aware that some children have food allergies that can be dangerous. Know your children, and consult with parents about allergies your kids may have. Also be sure to read food labels carefully as hidden ingredients can cause allergy problems.

## "Hide a Coin" Craft

Say: **God loves and cares for each of us. When the woman lost one of her**

coins, her collection was not complete! Nine coins were not enough. She wanted the missing one, too. Let's make a coin to remind us that the woman wanted every one of her coins. In the same way, God wants each one of us to be saved. God wants to be *your* friend!

**PARABLE POINT**

Give each child a small paper plate, a square of aluminum foil, and an unsharpened pencil. Show kids how to place the paper plate in the center of the foil, then fold the foil toward the center of the plate. Help kids fold the edges around the plate into a circular shape. Then, demonstrate how to gently press the unsharpened end of the pencil in the foil to make line and dot impressions. Encourage kids to decorate their projects to look like coins. Write children's names on their projects so you can send them home at the end of class.

As you help children with their crafts, talk with them about the joy of being part of God's family. Because God is our friend, we know that he watches over us, provides what we need, forgives our sins, and promises we will be with him forever. Collect the completed crafts, and set them aside until children are ready to go home.

## "Hidden Coin" Game

**Teacher Tip**

Exuberance in play may make it hard for some young children to keep their eyes closed. Other children may point out where they've hidden the coin as soon as the group begins to look for it. These breakdowns in "rules" will not hamper the fun children have in playing the game. To keep the game moving quickly, help children hide or find the coin if it seems that too much time has elapsed.

Say: **What do you think the woman said when she found her coin?** Affirm answers, then say: **We're going to play a Hide-and-Seek game to find one of our story coins. When we find the coin, we're going to shout, "God wants to be your friend!" Then everyone will cheer. Let's practice.** Lead the children in shouting, "God wants to be your friend!" and cheer several times.

Choose one child to hide the coin while the rest of the children close their eyes. When the coin is hidden, call that child back to the group, and have children open their eyes. Have children search the room to find the coin. Help the child who finds the coin remember to shout, "God wants to be your friend!" Encourage the rest of the class to jump and cheer.

Gather children together again, and have the finder hide the coin while remaining children close their eyes. Be ready to offer ideas for suitable places to hide the coin. Keep the game moving quickly so that many children will have opportunities to find and hide the coin. Be sure each child has a turn at hiding the coin.

# Together Prayer: Jump for Joy

Say:  God wants to be your friend. That is great news! In fact, it is such great news, we want to jump for joy. As we pray, let's think of some reasons we can jump for joy. When we jump and cheer, we praise God for loving us and caring for us.

Encourage children to jump and cheer as you pray, thanking God for his friendship and the good things he has done for us.

**Dear God,**

**When the woman found her coin…she jumped for joy!**

**When she told her friends how happy she was…they jumped for joy!**

**When we remember you sent Jesus to save us…we jump for joy!**

**When we are thankful for our families…we jump for joy!**

**When we know**  **God wants to be our friend…we jump for joy!**

**Thank you, God, for being our friend and loving us! Hooray! Amen!**

**PARABLE POINT**

# Parable of the Talents

## PARABLE POINT You Can Serve God
### Matthew 25:14-30

In this lesson you'll help your preschoolers discover that they can serve God as together you explore the parable of the talents.

• • • • • • • • • • • • • • • • • • • • • • • • • • • • • • • • • • • • • •

## A Message From Mary

Sometimes our sweet little ones can feel like they aren't very useful. It seems like they need Mommy and Daddy for everything. You get to help them realize God thinks they can do special things already!

"Don't Dig a Hole" is one of my favorite songs. It's fun to see the light bulb in kids' brains go on when they discover how God can use what they can do. Something that's tiny in our hands can be used for eternity in God's kingdom. We all have gifts and talents, and it's important that the children know they can be used for God's glory. After all, you are using your gifts by teaching them these wonderful stories. You're not burying your talent in the ground, and I want to thank you for your faithfulness!

• • • • • • • • • • • • • • • • • • • • • • • • • • • • • • • • • • • • • •

## Supply List

❑ Bible

❑ CD player

❑ *Simple Stories Jesus Told* CD (track 5)

❑ large container (approximately 8 quarts)

❑ 10-pound bag of rice

❑ plastic spoons

❑ 2 large baskets

❑ several seed packets

❑ wooden blocks

❑ paper play money

❑ disposable cups of water

❑ blueberries

❑ vanilla yogurt

❑ disposable cups

❑ construction paper strips (1x8-inch)

❑ paper plates

❑ stapler

❑ crayons

❑ napkins

❑ masking tape

# Welcoming Activity: Can You Dig It?

Before children arrive, fill the large container with uncooked rice. Hide three small wooden blocks in the rice. Have spoons available for digging.

After you've warmly welcomed preschoolers, gather them around the container and ask: **Do you like to dig? Have you ever found something interesting when you were digging?** Acknowledge responses, then continue: **Let's see if there's anything interesting buried in this rice.** Choose two or three children at a time to dig in the rice and find the blocks. Bury the blocks again, and give other children a turn. While children are playing, ask:

- **What do people usually do with blocks?**
- **What things do you like to make with blocks?**
- **How do you feel when you build?**

Say: **If we left these blocks buried in the rice, we couldn't build with them. If we want to use them, we can't hide them!**

When all have had turns, gather the children together on the floor.

Say: **I'm glad you helped me dig up these blocks. I need them to tell our Bible story. If we left them buried in the container, I wouldn't have them to tell the story.**

**Today we're going to hear a story Jesus told about a man who buried something. He dug a hole and hid something in the ground! Sometimes people think they don't have anything special that God can use, but we're going to learn that each one of us is important, and with our special abilities,  we can serve God!** Remove the blocks, and place the rice tub and one spoon where they can be used to tell the parable.

## Teacher Tip

You can make play money by cutting green paper into bill shapes and drawing dollar signs on them.

**PARABLE POINT**

# Parable Discovery:
## Parable of the Talents

Before class, prepare the props needed to tell the story. Put the seed packets in one basket. Put wooden blocks in the other. Place a chair, the play money, and the rice tub nearby.

Sit in a chair and gather children in front of you. Show children your open Bible. Say: **Jesus told this story, and we can read it in our Bibles in the book of Matthew.** Choose four children to act out the parable as you tell it using the following script.

## Teacher Tip

Containers that hold about eight quarts include wash basins, medium-sized plastic storage containers, punch bowls, or soup kettles. If your class is large, form several groups of children, and provide more than one container of rice.

**Once there was a man who was going away on a long trip.** Give eight "dollars" of play money to the child playing the part of the Owner.

**The Owner called three of his Helpers and told them to take care of his money while he was gone. He gave the First Helper five dollars.** Encourage children to count aloud as you help the Owner give five "dollars" to one child.

**He gave the Second Helper two dollars.** Count aloud as the Owner gives two "dollars" to the second child.

**And he gave the Third Helper one dollar.** Count with the children as the Owner gives one "dollar" to the third child.

**Then the Owner went away on his trip. While he was gone, the Helpers took care of the money. Here is what they did:**

**The First Helper used his money to earn more money. Maybe he bought some seeds.** Take the child's money, and hand the child the basket with the seeds. Encourage the child to act out what you describe, pausing for the child to do the actions. **He planted the seeds, watered them, pulled the weeds, and waited. Lots of vegetables grew! He picked the vegetables, put them in his basket, and sold them at the market. He spent five dollars on the seeds and earned ten dollars when he sold the vegetables!** Take the basket, thank the child for his vegetables, and encourage children to count with you as you place ten "dollars" into the child's hand. **Good job! Sit down and take a rest!**

**The Second Helper used his money to make more money. Perhaps he bought some wood.** Take the money from the second child, and give this child the basket of wooden blocks. Encourage the child to act out the part, providing the chair as a prop when needed. **He sawed the wood, hammered the wood, and made a chair. He sanded the chair smooth, painted it, and took it to the market to sell. He spent two dollars on the wood and earned four dollars when he sold the chair!** Take the chair, thank the child, and encourage children to count with you as you place four "dollars" into the child's hand. **Good job! Sit down and take a rest!**

**The Third Helper did not use his money to make more money. He thought, "One dollar is not much. Nobody can do anything with just one dollar. I'll just keep this money safe while my master is gone." So he dug a hole in the ground and buried his piece of money in the dirt!** Encourage the child to dig and bury the money in the rice tub. **Aww! That's sad! Then he took a nap.**

**After a long time, the Owner came home, called his Helpers together, and asked for his money.** Have the actors join you to finish the story. **The First Helper said, "You gave me five dollars to use, and now I have ten!"** Have the child give the Owner the money. **The Second Helper said, "You gave me two dollars to use, and now I have four!"** Have the child give the Owner the money. **The Third Helper said, "I didn't think anyone could use just one dollar, so I buried it in the ground."** Have the Third Helper pull his dollar from the rice tub.

**The Owner was happy with the Helpers who used what they had, but he was sad that the third man didn't use his money. Even small things are important if we use them wisely.** Thank your actors, and have them sit down.

God has given us many things besides money. He made each of us with special abilities. An *ability* is something you can do well. For example, you have the ability to hug, help, sing, and share. Just as the first two helpers used the money, we can use our abilities to serve God. God is happy when we use what we have to serve him. So don't hide your special abilities! Use them to serve God.

Discuss these questions with children.

• **What are special things you can do?**

• **How could you use those abilities to serve God?**

Say: **Those are wonderful abilities God has given you! Jesus told this story so we would remember to use what we have for God, even if it seems small. Whether your abilities are big or small, you can serve God!**

**PARABLE POINT**

# Sing and Celebrate:
## "Don't Dig a Hole" (track 5)

This fun song has a great beat that will get kids moving…and digging! As you lead this song, lead children in these actions during the chorus:

• As kids sing the chorus, have them pretend to dig during the singing of one line, then wag one finger back and forth during the next line. Alternate these actions throughout the chorus.

• Encourage kids to move with the music during the verses. Let them march, skip, or sway in whatever manner the music inspires.

# "Don't Dig a Hole"

*(Chorus)*

Don't dig a hole, dig-a-dig a hole,

Don't dig a hole and bury it.

Don't dig a hole, dig-a-dig a hole,

Don't dig a hole and bury it.

*(Repeat.)*

The first guy was wise.

He knew how to invest.

He made ten from five,

And then he took a rest. (Oh, yes!)

*(Repeat chorus.)*

The second guy had talents.

He knew just what to do.

He doubled God's money:

There were four instead of two.

(And they grew!)

*(Repeat chorus.)*

The third guy did nothing.

He buried it that day.

He only had one talent,

But he threw it all away.

*(Repeat chorus.)*

Don't dig a hole in the ground.

## "Bury the Berry" Snack

Have kids wash hands before eating (or use wet wipes). Drop a single blueberry into each individual serving cup, then fill the cups with vanilla yogurt. Choose some children to serve others by distributing snacks and cups of water. Others can set out spoons and napkins. Still others can serve by helping clean up. Affirm children as they use their talents of friendship and helpfulness to serve God and others.

Tell children they can search for the berry treat you've buried in their yogurt. As children eat, ask about things they like to do. Help them think of ways they can use these talents or abilities for God. Small children are dependent in many ways and need help to discover the things they are able to do unassisted. Help them recognize that when they help with tasks, give hugs, sing, share, or form friendships because they belong to Jesus, they are serving God.

## Allergy Alert

Be aware that some children have food allergies that can be dangerous. Know your children, and consult with parents about allergies your kids may have. Also be sure to read food labels carefully as hidden ingredients can cause allergy problems.

## "Use It for God" Pouch

Before class, cut colorful strips of construction paper (1x8-inch). Give each child a paper plate and two strips of construction paper. Provide crayons, and tell kids to draw pictures on both sides of the plate showing things they can do to serve God. Remember to put names on the crafts so children can take them home at the end of class. To finish the project, fold the plate in half, and help children staple the two strips onto the plate to serve as handles for the pouch.

While kids are working, say: **You are growing every day, and there are many things you can do to serve God. Tell me about the things you like to do. How can you serve God with that ability?** Listen to answers, and help children expand their awareness of both their independence and their ability to serve God and others. **This pouch will help you remember to not hide your abilities away, but instead remember you can serve God.**

**PARABLE POINT**

## "Run, Jump, and Tell" Games

Form two relay teams. With masking tape, designate a starting line and a finish line at opposite ends of the room. Place wooden blocks along the finish line, and set an empty basket nearby. The goal of this relay is not competition, but participation. Help those who need it so that everyone completes the race. Be sure to clear the area of chairs or other obstacles, and allow enough room between teams so children play safely. Play "Don't Dig a Hole" (track 5) in the background as children play.

Say: **The first game is called "Run to Help." When it is your turn, run to the finish line, pick up one wooden block and put it in the basket, then run back to your team. Then it is the next child's turn.** Give a signal for teams to start, and cheer each one's efforts. When all have had a turn, say: **You can hurry and help others. That is one way you can serve God.**

**PARABLE POINT**

The second game is "Jump for Joy." When it is your turn, jump to the finish line, shout "I love Jesus!" and jump back to your team. Then it is the next child's turn to jump. When all have had turns, say: **You can use your voice to praise God. That is another way** 🐵 **you can serve God.**

**PARABLE POINT** 🐵

The third game is "Hurry to Love." When it is your turn, hurry to the finish line, give the teacher a big hug, and then hurry back to your team. Give the next child a hug, and then it is his or her turn. When everyone has had a turn, say: **You can show love to others. That is another way** 🐵 **you can serve God.**

**PARABLE POINT** 🐵

## Together Prayer: Serving God

Often we think of prayer as something we say, but children can also express themselves to God actively, using their bodies. Help children use their bodies in this prayer activity.

Say: **God made you in a wonderful way. There are so many things you can do! Let's thank God for the ways we can serve him. When I pray about a way to serve God, do the actions with me.**

**Dear God,** *(Fold hands and bow head.)*

**Thank you for all the things we can do. We can run to help others.** *(Run in place.)* **We can jump up and praise you.** *(Jump and shout, "Yea, God!")* **We can tell others about your love.** *(Hug a friend and say, "Jesus loves you!")* **Help us use all these great abilities to serve you.** *(Fold hands and bow head.)* **Amen.**

# Parable of the Persistent Neighbor

## PARABLE POINT We Can Pray

### Luke 11:5-10

"Knock and the door will be opened to you." What a promise! In this lesson preschoolers will discover through the parable of the persistent neighbor that we can pray to God anytime—even if it's midnight!

• • • • • • • • • • • • • • • • • • • • • • • • • • • • • • • • • • • • •

## A Message From Mary

Do you ever pray and wonder if your prayers are being heard? Well, this is a great story of tenacity. It's a story of how we <u>all</u> should pray—never giving up, never giving in, and not settling for crumbs when we can knock on the door and get the whole loaf! So that is what you want to share with these little ones: Keep on praying to Jesus, for he hears every single prayer.

The importance of persistence and "waiting" on the Lord is not an easy lesson for children (or even us older children!) to learn. But the benefits of asking, seeking, and knocking as the Bible says far outweigh anything the world has to offer.

Thank you for being so faithful and praying with these little ones God has entrusted you with. As the Bible says, "I have no greater joy than to hear that my children are walking in the truth" (3 John 4). So don't give up praying. God will reward you.

*Mary Brackett*

• • • • • • • • • • • • • • • • • • • • • • • • • • • • • • • • • • • • •

## Supply List

- ❑ CD player
- ❑ *Simple Stories Jesus Told* CD (track 6)
- ❑ Bible
- ❑ brown paper
- ❑ tape
- ❑ 1 banana, 1 orange
- ❑ 1 empty, clean pint or quart milk carton per child
- ❑ craft knife
- ❑ stapler
- ❑ rubber bands
- ❑ Teddy Grahams snack crackers
- ❑ disposable cups of water
- ❑ loaf of bread
- ❑ clear plastic bag with a piece of bread, sealed with a twist tie
- ❑ masking tape
- ❑ markers
- ❑ napkins

# Welcoming Activity: Knock, Knock!

Before children arrive, place a banana, an orange, and a loaf of bread close by. Ask the children to sit on the floor in front of you. Begin by saying: **Hello! I'm so glad you're here today! I have a joke for you. Ready?**

**Teacher:** Knock, knock!

**Children:** Who's there?

**Teacher:** Banana. *(Hold up the banana.)*

**Children:** Banana who?

*(Repeat this sequence three or four times. Then continue.)*

**Teacher:** Knock, knock!

**Children:** Who's there?

**Teacher:** Orange. *(Hold up the orange.)*

**Children:** Orange who?

**Teacher:** Orange you glad I didn't say *banana?*

Say: **Were you relieved or glad when I finally stopped saying** *banana?* Let the children respond. **When I was telling you that joke, I kept saying the same thing over and over and over again. Sometimes that can be really annoying! Have you ever asked your mom or dad for something over and over and over again?** Give the children a few minutes to discuss this. **When you ask for something a lot and don't give up, that's called being persistent. Sometimes, when you are persistent, the person will give you what you ask, just so you'll stop bugging him or her!**

Make a ringing sound. Pick up the banana as if it were a phone. Say into the banana phone: **Hello. What? No! Please don't bother me. My children are with me, and we're in the middle of class. I can't get up and give you some bread. Goodbye!** Pretend to "hang up" the banana.

**Anyway, Jesus told a story about…** Make the ringing sound again. Pick up the banana and say: **Hello. You again? Will you please stop bothering me? I already told you, I can't give you anything. No, absolutely not! Goodbye!** Pretend to "hang up" the banana.

**I'm sorry. As I was saying, Jesus told a story about a person who kept bugging his neighbor for some bread in the middle of the night.** Make a ringing sound again. Pick up the banana and say: **Hello. Ahhhh! Not you again. OK,**

**what do you want? Fine! I'll give you some bread if you'll stop calling me in the middle of class!** Put down the banana phone. Pick up the loaf of bread, and walk to the door. Pretend to hand it to someone. Then come and sit down.

**Wow! That guy is really persistent! He kept asking me for bread, so I finally gave it to him just so he'd stop pestering me!**

**Today, we're going to hear a story that Jesus told about a person who was also persistent. Jesus told this story to remind us that**  **we can pray to God anytime and that we should be persistent when we pray.**

**PARABLE POINT**

## Parable Discovery:
## Parable of the Persistent Neighbor

Before class, make a "door" out of brown paper, and tape it to a wall.

Have the children sit near the door you've made. Open your Bible to Luke 11:5-10. Show the children your open Bible.

Say: **We're going to hear the story that Jesus told of the persistent neighbor. I'll be the person who's asleep, and you can help tell the story by being the neighbor who comes to ask for bread in the middle of the night.**

**A friend was asleep in his home. At midnight his neighbor knocked on his door and said, "Friend, lend me three loaves of bread because I have a visitor and nothing to give him to eat!" But the one who was asleep answered, "Don't bother me. The door is locked and my children and I are sleeping. I can't get up and give you anything."** Ask for one child to come and knock on the door while you pretend to sleep. Ham it up with snoring and other sound effects.

**Neighbor:** *(Knocking on the door)* Can you give me bread, please?

**Teacher:** No! I'm sleeping. Go away!

*(Repeat this a few times, allowing several children to be the neighbor. Then continue.)*

**Neighbor:** *(Knocking on the door)* Can you give me bread, please?

**Teacher:** OK! I'll give it to you so you'll stop bothering me!

Say: **Jesus finished his story by saying, "Ask and it will be given to you; seek and you will find; knock and the door will be opened to you. For everyone who asks**

receives; he who seeks finds; and to him who knocks, the door will be opened." Jesus wasn't talking here about real doors or bread, but he was explaining that  we can pray. He was encouraging people to be persistent in praying and in asking for God to come and help them.  We can pray, too, even if it's midnight!

## Three-in-One:
## House, Guitar, and Puppet Theater

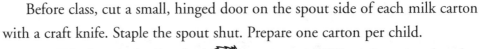

Before class, cut a small, hinged door on the spout side of each milk carton with a craft knife. Staple the spout shut. Prepare one carton per child.

Say: **We're learning today that**  **we can pray! We're going to make a handy little craft today that we'll use both for our snack time and for our song time. You can take this house with you to help you remember that we can be persistent in prayer, just like the neighbor was persistent in asking his friend for bread.**

Give each child a milk carton and a strip of masking tape. Be sure each child's name is written on his or her carton.

Encourage children to tear the tape into smaller pieces and to cover most of the outside of the carton with masking tape "shingles." When they are finished, they can decorate the shingles with markers. Finally, have each child add three rubber bands around the top of the carton to create a guitar. Save these Three-in-One Houses for snack and song times.

## Sing and Celebrate:
## "At Midnight" (track 6)

Have children use their Three-in-One crafts while you play the song. They can pluck at the rubber bands as if they're guitar strings. Include these motions:
- Each time the song says "knock," have children knock on the sides of their "guitars" or make one fist knock on the palm of the other hand.
- Every time the lyrics say "midnight," have children yawn and stretch.

Then say: **Jesus told the story about the persistent neighbor who came knocking at midnight to remind us that we can "knock" on God's door anytime. He is always awake and ready to listen to our prayers. Being persistent in prayer teaches us to be patient and to pray all the time.**

## "At Midnight"

(La, la, la, la, la, la, la, la, la)

I heard a knock at my front door.

What is my neighbor knocking for?

Maybe he thinks I'm a grocery store.

Why does he come at midnight?

Why does he come at midnight?

He said, "I need three loaves of bread.

I don't wanna wake ya from your bed.

But my guests, they need to be fed.

Can you help me at midnight?

Can you help me at midnight?"

*(Chorus)*

At first I turned him away,

But then I said, "Oh, it's OK.

Your persistence makes me say,

'I'll help you at midnight.

I'll help you at midnight.' "

So keep on asking every day,

'Cause God will hear the words you pray.

He will bless you, come what may,

Even if it's midnight,

Even if it's midnight.

*(Repeat chorus.)*

So keep on asking, on and on,

Even when the sun is gone.

Be faithful and so strong,

Even if it's midnight,

Even if it's midnight.

(La, la, la, la, la, la, la, la, la)

# Loaves for a Neighbor

Have each child sit with a friend. Hand out cups of water and the Three-in-One Houses. Give each child a napkin with some Teddy Grahams snack crackers and a piece of bread.

Have children rip the bread up into small "loaves." Next, ask them to take turns with their partners telling the story of the persistent neighbor using the Teddy Grahams as the neighbors and the ripped bread as loaves of bread. They can use their carton houses as miniature theaters for their edible puppetry. When children have had fun playing, they can eat their snacks.

# Allergy Alert

Be aware that some children have food allergies that can be danger-ous. Know your children, and consult with parents about allergies your kids may have. Also be sure to read food labels carefully as hidden ingredients can cause allergy problems.

## Drop the Bread Bag

**PARABLE POINT**

### Teacher Tip

Game time is a great time to rein-force the point of the lesson! If you wish, you may vary what The Friend says. For example, other phrases may include: "Ask, seek, knock," or "Be per-sistent in prayer," or "Knock, the door will be opened." You may be surprised at how often these phrases will pop up in your mind throughout the rest of the day!

Have the children sit cross-legged in a circle on the floor with their hands folded like they are praying. Choose one child to be The Friend. Hand that child a clear plastic bag containing one piece of bread. The bag should be sealed with a twist tie.

The Friend walks around the circle behind the children's backs. As this child walks, he or she says, "We can pray." Quietly the child drops the bread bag behind one child and walks quickly around the outside of the circle, trying to sit down in the spot where the bag was dropped. The one who has the bag dropped behind him or her needs to get up, grab the bag, and try to tag The Friend before The Friend takes his or her spot!

Play until each child has had a chance to be The Friend.

## "Knock, Knock" Prayer

Have the children sit in two lines facing each other. Center the lines near the door that you used earlier in the lesson.

Say: **We can ask God for help any time of day or night! Let's think of things we can ask God to help us with.** Take a few minutes to brainstorm ideas with the children.

**Let's take turns going up to the door. Each of you can knock on the door and then say, "Dear God, please help me_____." I'll begin and end the prayer.**

**Dear God,**

**Thank you that we can pray! What a privilege and a blessing to know that you hear us no matter what time of day or night. Thank you, too, for your promise through Jesus that if we ask, seek, and knock on your door of prayer, that you will answer us.**

Encourage each child to go up to the door, knock, and say, "Dear God, please help me to…" If a child feels uncomfortable with this, let the child just say "Thank you, God" from his or her seat.

Finish the prayer by saying: **Help us all to be persistent in prayer. In Jesus' name, amen.**

# Parable of the Yeast

**PARABLE POINT** With Jesus We Can Do Big Things
Matthew 13:33

Through the parable of the yeast, preschoolers will learn that even though they are little, with Jesus they can do big things!

● ● ● ● ● ● ● ● ● ● ● ● ● ● ● ● ● ● ● ● ● ● ● ● ● ● ● ● ● ● ● ● ● ● ● ● ● ● ● ● ● ● ● ●

## A Message From Mary

I will never forget the story my mom told about the first cherry pie that she made for my dad. She accidentally bought the wrong ingredients and made the whole pie with maraschino cherries. Yuck!!! Fortunately for her, everyone just laughed, and she turned out to be a great cook after all.

Not all of us have experiences like that. But if we leave out the yeast in our bread, it certainly doesn't rise. I know if I don't start every day with Jesus, my life is kind of flat, just like it talks about in this song, "Lord I Need You." We need Jesus in our lives. There is nothing more important to teach our children, and this parable is a great illustration of that.

From the bread that you bake and the songs that you sing to the stories that you read, you are sharing the love of Jesus. Thank you! You'll never know what God might have cooked up for you!

● ● ● ● ● ● ● ● ● ● ● ● ● ● ● ● ● ● ● ● ● ● ● ● ● ● ● ● ● ● ● ● ● ● ● ● ● ● ● ●

## Supply List

- ❑ CD player
- ❑ *Simple Stories Jesus Told* CD (track 7)
- ❑ Bible
- ❑ 2 clear plastic 1-liter bottles
- ❑ sugar, yeast, and warm water
- ❑ whisk and measuring spoons
- ❑ 1 cracker
- ❑ 1 slice of bread
- ❑ paper towels
- ❑ resealable plastic bags
- ❑ uncooked white rice
- ❑ food coloring
- ❑ peppermint extract

- ❑ 1 lemon
- ❑ bowls of miniature snack items such as tiny crackers, miniature chocolate chips, raisins, or small cereal pieces
- ❑ disposable cups of water
- ❑ paper towel tube
- ❑ sandpaper
- ❑ safety scissors
- ❑ crayons
- ❑ spoons
- ❑ photocopies of "Mini Mixture Tag" (p. 53)
- ❑ tape

# Welcoming Activity: Secret Ingredient

**Teacher Tip**

Each time you change to a new activity, direct the children's attention to the bottles and have them check on what's happening with the experiment. After about ten minutes or so, the water containing the yeast will have bubbled over the top! (Be sure to put a few paper towels under the yeast bottle.)

**PARABLE POINT**

Before the children arrive, set out the following items on a small table that can be clearly seen by the children: two clear plastic 1-liter bottles with the tops cut off and the labels removed, half a cup of sugar, a tablespoon of yeast, a pitcher of warm water, measuring spoons, paper towels, and a whisk.

Invite the children to sit on the floor near the table. Say: **I'm so glad you're here! We have a tiny little story today about a tiny little thing that makes a *big* difference! But first we're going to do an experiment. Each one of you will get to help. I'll call you up one at a time to set up our experiment.**

Put the bottles side by side. Ask each child to help with one of the following tasks. Fill each bottle half way up with warm water. Add 2 tablespoons of sugar to each bottle. Using the wire whisk, stir each bottle of sugar-water until the sugar dissolves. Then say: **So far we've done the same thing to each bottle, right? But now, we're going to add a tiny bit of a secret ingredient to one of the bottles, and we'll see what happens!** Ask one child to add 1 tablespoon of yeast to one of the bottles. Whisk the yeast in until it has dissolved.

**We're going to let these two bottles sit for a while, and we'll check back later to see what's happening to them. In the meantime, I'm going to tell you one of the tiniest parables that Jesus ever told! He told this story to let us know that**  **with Jesus we can do big things!**

# Parable Discovery:
## Parable of the Yeast

Before children arrive, set a table nearby so that you can reach all of the "five senses" examples of things that are little but powerful. Also have a cracker and a slice of bread nearby.

Ask the children to sit in a circle on the floor. Open your Bible to Matthew 13:33. Show the children your open Bible. Say: **Our story today is very, very short! In fact, it's one of the shortest parables that Jesus told.**

**In this Bible verse, Jesus said that the kingdom of heaven is like yeast that a woman took and mixed into a large amount of flour until it worked all through the dough. That's it!**

Hold up one saltine cracker and one slice of bread. Say: **Look how big this bread is compared to this cracker. Do you know what the difference is? Just a little bit of yeast! The cracker is made of flour and water, but the bread has a little bit of yeast that went through the whole batch of dough to make it get light and fluffy. Yeast is the little secret ingredient we added to our bottle.**

**Jesus is saying that even though yeast is little, it does big things. Jesus wanted the people to know his love is powerful and that  with Jesus we can do big things!**

**Let's use our five senses to discover what other things are little, but powerful. First, what are our five senses?** Give the children time to list sight, smell, hearing, taste, and touch. Say: **Great! I'm going to pass some things around the circle that are little, but powerful. Let's begin with our sense of sight.**

### Sight

**Let's use our eyes to see something that is small, but powerful.** Hold up a resealable plastic bag with two cups of white rice inside. Add three or four drops of food coloring to the bag. Point out how tiny the drops are compared with the big amount of rice. Close the bag securely. Pass it around the circle, and let each child gently shake it a few times. After several minutes, children will see colored rice.

### Smell

**Now, let's use our noses to smell something that is small, but powerful.** Put a few drops of peppermint extract on a paper towel, and put it in a plastic bag. Again, point out that you only used a few drops of this liquid to make a powerful smell. Pass it around the circle, and encourage the children to take a sniff.

### Hearing

**Now, let's use our ears to hear something that is small, but powerful.** Tell the children you are going to use a quiet whisper to talk to them through a paper towel tube. Walk around the circle and whisper in each child's ear,  "With Jesus we can do big things." When everyone has heard, ask the children to repeat what you said out loud.

### Taste

**Now, let's use our tongues to taste something that is small, but powerful.** Go around the circle and squeeze a tiny drop of lemon onto each child's tongue. As you squeeze, have the child close his or her eyes in case the lemon sprays juice!

*Touch*

**Let's use our fingers to feel something that is small, but powerful.** Pass around the circle a couple small squares of rough sandpaper. Encourage the children to feel how rough a few grains of sand can be. Explain that sandpaper can do big things, even though it is little.

**PARABLE POINT**

Finish by saying: **All of these things are small but powerful! The parable of the yeast can remind us that even though you are little,  with Jesus you can do big things. Let's think of some big things that God can help you do.** Give the children time to think and share. Ideas may include: sharing (even when it's hard), encouraging others, helping at home, obeying parents and teachers, or being patient. Reassure the children that these are big, difficult things to do—even for adults! But with Jesus' help, even though they are little, they can do these big things.

# Sing and Celebrate:
## "Lord I Need You" (track 7)

● ● ● ● ● ● ● ● ● ● ● ● ● ● ● ● ● ● ● ● ● ● ● ● ● ● ● ● ● ● ● ●

This song is great for starting small and getting big! During the verses of the song, let children clap or act as if they are making bread. When the chorus begins, have children squat close to the floor, then "grow" bigger and taller until they're reaching to the ceiling. Repeat these actions during the remainder of the song.

**PARABLE POINT**

Say: **Little by little,  with Jesus we can do big things!**

## "Lord I Need You"

I was making bread with a little recipe,

But I forgot the yeast, and what did I see?

Well, my bread was flat, what do you think of that?

The smallest thing was the best thing that I need.

*(Chorus)*

Lord, I need you more every day.

From the moment I rise when I awake,

Little by little, I wanna say,

"Lord, I need you every day."

Just like that yeast in that good-smelling dough,

With all the right ingredients my bread will grow.

But God's love will rise above.

The light of his love will one day show.

*(Repeat chorus twice.)*

*(Repeat first verse.)*

I need you.

I need you.

## Mini Mixture

• • • • • • • • • • • • • • • • • • • • • • • • • • • • • • • • • • • • • • •

On a table, set out bowls of the miniature snacks and spoons or scoops. Give each child a resealable plastic bag. Allow the children to scoop their own bags of mini treats to nibble. Serve each child a cup of water as well.

After the children have eaten their mini snacks, ask them to go back and make another treat bag to give away. This bag will be used during the craft time.

 ## Allergy Alert

Be aware that some children have food allergies that can be dangerous. Know your children, and consult with parents about allergies your kids may have. Also be sure to read food labels carefully as hidden ingredients can cause allergy problems.

## Tiny Treats

• • • • • • • • • • • • • • • • • • • • • • • • • • • • • • • • • • • • • • •

Before class photocopy one Mini Mixture Tag (p. 53) for each child.

Say: **Today we learned that just like yeast we are little, but that with Jesus we can do big things. Here's a little gift that you can share with a friend or family member—to share God's love with that person. We're going to make a tag to put on the extra bag of Mini Mixture that you made to give away. You may want to give this to someone who doesn't know about Jesus yet.**

Set out safety scissors and crayons. Help the children to cut out their tags and decorate them. Be sure each child's name is on his or her gift project. Next, help each child tape the tag onto a Mini Mixture bag.

# Big Results

## For Extra Fun!

This game is sure to result in lots of laughter! After you have tried the first game, try this variation: Have each child perform each action. For example, clap once, then have the whole group clap once. See if everyone can keep up with all the motions. Be sure to point out that although each person added just one tiny motion, in the end it turned into a *big* thing!

Have children stand in a circle. Say: **We're going to use our bodies to show how something that starts out small can make big things happen! Here's how it works: I'll start by doing just one motion, let's say a clap. Then we'll go around the circle and each person can add one more motion. Each time we'll start with my motion and do each one in order; that will help us remember them all. In the end, we'll try the whole thing together. Are you ready? Let's begin!**

Here's an example:

Teacher: Clap once.

Child 1: Clap once, spin around.

Child 2: Clap once, spin around, stomp feet.

Child 3: Clap once, spin around, stomp feet, shout "hooray!"

## Each One Tell One

Before you end in prayer, take one last chance to look at the yeast experiment. By now there should be at least two to three inches of foam on the yeast bottle. Then ask the children to sit on the floor facing you.

Say: **Jesus told us that even though yeast is tiny, it can powerfully work through a whole batch of bread. The same is true of you! Even though you are still small,**  **with Jesus you can do big things.**

**One big thing you can do is to tell others about Jesus. If each person tells just one person, God's kingdom will grow and grow, just like the yeast did in this bottle.**

**Let's do an "Each One Tell One" prayer. I'll begin by saying, "Dear Jesus, I need you and so does [name of a child]."**

**When you hear your name, come up and link arms with me. Then that child will say the same thing, and so on, until we're all linked together.**

End the prayer by saying: **Thank you that**  **with Jesus we can do big things! In Jesus name, amen.**

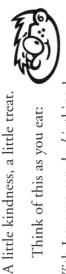

## Mini Mixture Tag

A little kindness, a little treat.

Think of this as you eat:

With Jesus we can do *big* things!

Love,

## Mini Mixture Tag

A little kindness, a little treat.

Think of this as you eat:

With Jesus we can do *big* things!

Love,

## Mini Mixture Tag

A little kindness, a little treat.

Think of this as you eat:

With Jesus we can do *big* things!

Love,

## Mini Mixture Tag

A little kindness, a little treat.

Think of this as you eat:

With Jesus we can do *big* things!

Love,

# Parable of the Rich Fool

## PARABLE POINT We Can Share
### Luke 12:16-21

What does it mean to be "rich toward God"? In the parable of the rich fool, preschoolers will learn that sharing, not storing, is God's desire for us.

• • • • • • • • • • • • • • • • • • • • • • • • • • • • • • • • • • • • •

## A Message From Mary

One of the first words we hear our children say is "mine" or "more." It can be hard to teach our children to share in a society that prides itself in accumulating things.

That's why this is such a great story. Jesus' parable is about a guy who has everything backward. Instead of God, <u>things</u> have come to rule his life. Like the guy says in the background of my song, "Gimme! Gimme!" But his things don't love him or care about him.

What a great opportunity you have. Through the story of the rich fool, you can teach the importance of learning what it means to share. As the children see your life and the love you share with them, they will learn to do the same.

God bless you for seeing that the treasure you seek comes not from the things you keep, but through the love that you give.

• • • • • • • • • • • • • • • • • • • • • • • • • • • • • • • • • • •

## Supply List

- ❏ CD player
- ❏ *Simple Stories Jesus Told* CD (track 8)
- ❏ Bible
- ❏ cup, cereal bowl, and larger bowl
- ❏ box of cereal
- ❏ 4 empty, clean 1-liter bottles with lids
- ❏ uncooked rice or beans
- ❏ 1-quart resealable bags
- ❏ paper fasteners
- ❏ ice cream or vanilla yogurt
- ❏ frozen limeade concentrate
- ❏ bananas
- ❏ milk
- ❏ disposable cups
- ❏ sturdy paper plates
- ❏ small, wax-coated paper cups
- ❏ scissors
- ❏ photocopies of smoothie recipe (p. 61)
- ❏ hole punch
- ❏ toys
- ❏ string or ribbon

# Welcoming Activity:
## Bigger Barn Builder

Before children arrive, set a small table near the story area. Place the cup and bowls on the table along with one box of cereal. Clear containers are ideal for this activity since the children can see better what's going on, but are not required.

Ask the children to sit on the floor so they can see the table. Tell them you're glad they came. Pour the cereal into the cup until it overflows. Munch on the cereal that spills, but don't share any…yet! Say: **Oh, dear! This cup isn't big enough to hold all *my* cereal. Maybe I'll try a bowl.**

Pour the small cup of cereal into the smaller of the two bowls. Add more cereal from the box until it overflows. Keep eating the cereal as it spills. Feel free to make comments like: "This is great!" or "Wow! What yummy food." Say: **Oh, my! This bowl isn't big enough to hold all *my* cereal either. Maybe I'll try a bigger container.**

Pour the bowl of cereal into the larger bowl. Add more cereal from the box until it overflows. Munch on the cereal that spills. Say: **Oh, dear! This bowl isn't big enough to hold all *my* cereal either. I wonder what I should do?** It's likely that one of the children will suggest sharing the cereal! If they don't, make the suggestion yourself.

Pass out small cups of cereal for the kids to eat. As they eat, say: **What a great suggestion you had to *share*! Today we're going to hear a story that Jesus told about a man who was blessed with lots and lots of stuff, but instead of sharing, he just kept building bigger barns in which to store all of his stuff! We'll find out what happened to him in a minute, but Jesus told this story to teach us that  we can share!**

 **Allergy Alert**

Be aware that some children have food allergies that can be dangerous. Know your children, and consult with parents about allergies your kids may have. Also be sure to read food labels carefully as hidden ingredients can cause allergy problems.

# Parable Discovery:
## Parable of the Rich Fool

Have the children sit in a circle. You'll need several toys.

Before you begin the story, open your Bible to Luke 12:16-21. Show children

## For Extra Fun!

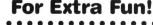

Almost any type of cereal works for this. Popcorn is a great choice, too, because of its volume. If you like, you can use more containers in graduated sizes. The children get a big kick out of this demonstration, especially as it becomes more ridiculous the longer it goes on! This is great for driving home the point.

**PARABLE POINT**

your open Bible. Say: **Jesus told a story that we call the parable of the rich fool. What does it mean to be rich?** Let the children answer. **Good. You're right! When someone is rich, it usually means that person has lots of money and lots of things, including food. Now, what does it mean to be a fool?** This may be more difficult. Give the children a few minutes to offer suggestions. **A fool is not very smart or wise. In our story today, we'll see that although the rich man had lots of stuff, he didn't have the most important thing he needed: God. If the rich man had been "rich toward God," he would have understood that all our stuff—or blessings—come from God. And God wants us to share.**

**We're going to act out the story of the rich fool. I'll point to you or tell you what to do or say as we go along. I'll need one person to be the Rich Fool.** Choose a child for this role, and give that child all the toys to hold. Then use the following script to tell the story:

*Teacher:* The farm of a certain rich man produced a good crop.

*(Point to the child who is the Rich Fool. Have this child stand, hold up an armload of toys, and say, "I've got lots of stuff!" Then the child may sit down.)*

*Teacher:* This man had barns where he stored his stuff.

*(Have the children squat in a circle as if they are a small barn. Let the Rich Fool walk around the edges of the barn while holding a bunch of toys.)*

*Teacher:* The rich man thought to himself, "What shall I do? I have no place to store my crops. My barns are too small."

*(Have the Rich Fool say, "I've got lots of stuff!" Then the child may sit down.)*

*Teacher:* Then the Rich Fool said, "This is what I'll do. I'll tear down my barns and build bigger ones, and there I will store all my grain and my stuff."

*(Have the children stand in a circle and stretch their arms up high as if they are a big barn. Let the Rich Fool walk around the edges of the barn while holding a bunch of toys.)*

*Teacher:* And then the Rich Fool said to himself, "I have plenty of good things to last for many years. I'll take life easy…eat, drink and be merry."

*(Have the Rich Fool say, "I've got lots of stuff!")*

*Teacher:* But God had something else in mind! God said to the Rich Fool, "You fool! This very night you will die. Then who will get all the stuff you have saved?"

*(Have the Rich Fool cover his or her eyes.)*

**Teacher:** The Rich Fool died that night. Jesus ended his story by saying that this is how it will be with anyone who stores up things for himself but is not rich toward God. If the Rich Fool had known God, he would have known that God wants us to be sharers. It's good to know that  we can share.

**PARABLE POINT**

## Sing and Celebrate: "Greedy Guy" (track 8)

Before children arrive, put about half a cup of uncooked rice or beans into each of the 1-liter bottles, and secure the lids on the bottles.

Help the children to stand in a circle. Show them the bottles and demonstrate how these can be shaken and used as noisemakers. Say: **Uh, oh! We have a problem. I only have four shakers for our song, but there are lots of you. Any ideas?** Let the children suggest sharing. **Great idea! I'll start the song, then every once in a while I'll call "share!" and you can pass your shaker to someone else in the circle. After you've had a turn with a shaker, sit down, and clap to the song. We'll do this a few times so that everyone can share the shakers!**

Play "Greedy Guy" (track 8), and let children shake the noisemakers and move to the music. Call out "share!" several times, and have children pass the shakers so that everyone gets a turn.

## "Greedy Guy"

There was a very greedy guy
Who thought he had so much.
He was rich, yet he was poor,
'Cause he said, "I don't have enough."
So he filled up his barn up to the brim,
But then he built a bigger barn.
But he did not share his crop with his
friends

Or invite them to his farm.

*(Chorus)*
'Cause you can be rich but very poor,
When you're always wanting for more.
You can be rich but very poor,
When you're always wanting for more.

The harvest came, but he didn't change.

He would always fuss and fume (Oh, pooh!)

About needing a storage space.

For his crops, he had to make room.

But one day he keeled over. (Uh!)

I think he might have died.

But the sad thing is that no one knew,

And no one even cried.

*(Repeat chorus.)*

So don't store up your treasures.

Set your mind on things above.

By our hearts, he'll measure

How we share God's love.

*(Last chorus)*

'Cause you can be rich but very poor,

When you're always wanting for more.

You can be rich but very poor,

When you're always wanting for more.

You can be rich but very poor,

When you're always wanting for more.

You can be rich but very poor,

But all we have, all we have,

All we have is from the Lord.

# Squish and Share Smoothie

Give each child a resealable plastic bag (quart size). Help them to add the following ingredients to each bag:

• 1 scoop (about ⅓ cup) of vanilla ice cream (vanilla yogurt can be used if you don't have access to a freezer)

• 1 teaspoon frozen limeade concentrate

• 1-inch slice of banana, peeled

• 1 tablespoon milk (omit if using yogurt)

Have an adult squeeze the air out of each bag and seal it securely. Have the children gently squish and shake the ingredients until mixed. Help the children clip a corner off their bags and squish the smoothies into cups.

Pair up the children. Ask them to enjoy their smoothies with their partners and to share their ideas about the following questions:

• **What was the best thing anyone ever shared with you?**

• **What has God given to you with that you can share with others?**

If you have time at the end, come together as a whole group, and ask children what they discussed.

## ! Allergy Alert

Be aware that some children have food allergies that can be danger-ous. Know your children, and consult with parents about allergies your kids may have. Also be sure to read food labels carefully as hidden ingredients can cause allergy problems.

## Serve and Share Platter

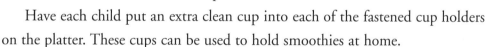

This is a fun make 'n' take platter that the children can use at home to serve Squish and Share Smoothies to their friends and family!

Before children arrive, cut the tops off of small, wax-coated paper cups until the cups are one inch tall. You'll need four cups per child. You'll also want to make one of the platters to show children as a sample.

Give each child a sturdy paper plate. Help children poke large paper fasteners (or "brads") into the bottoms of their cut paper cups. Next, put these cups on top of each plate, and poke the fasteners through the plate. Then fold the tips of the brads flat across the bottom of the plate.

Have each child put an extra clean cup into each of the fastened cup holders on the platter. These cups can be used to hold smoothies at home.

Punch one hole in the rim of each platter to attach the Squish and Share Smoothie Recipe (p. 61). Tie this on with a string or ribbon.

## Sharing Circle

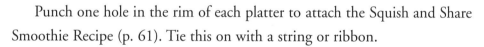

**PARABLE POINT**

Have the children sit on the floor in a circle. Give each child a small toy, book, or stuffed animal. Explain that you are going to play the song "Greedy Guy" (track 8), and that while the music is playing, they can play with the toy they have. When the music stops, they are to stop, say "We can share!" and pass that toy to the person on the right.

Play the song several times, stopping the music randomly so children can switch toys.

# Together Prayer: Rich Toward God

Encourage the children to fold their hands and bow their heads. Explain that you will say part of the prayer, and, if they wish, they can respond by saying, "Rich toward God" after each section.

**Dear God,**

**When we share our toys, we are...**

**Rich toward God!**

**When we share our money, we are...**

**Rich toward God!**

**When we understand that everything we have comes from you, we are...**

**Rich toward God!**

**When we love people more than our things, we are...**

**Rich toward God!**

**Help us to be sharers so that we can be...**

**Rich toward God!**

**In Jesus' name, amen.**

# Squish and Share Smoothie Recipe

**Makes 4 small smoothies**

Put the following ingredients into a 1-gallon resealable plastic bag:

- 4 scoops of vanilla ice cream or vanilla yogurt
- 4 teaspoons frozen limeade concentrate
- 1 banana, peeled and chopped into small chunks
- ⅓ cup milk (omit if using yogurt)

Squeeze the air out of the bag, and seal. Gently squish the ingredients until mixed. Clip a corner of the bag, and squish the smoothie into four small cups.

To serve, place the smoothies on the Serve and Share Platter. Serve to your friends and family.

As you enjoy your smoothie, discuss this question:

- **What has God given to you that you can share with others?**

Read Luke 12:16-21 together.

- - - - - - - - - - - - - - - - - - - - - - - - - - - - - - - - - - - - -

# Squish and Share Smoothie Recipe

**Makes 4 small smoothies**

Put the following ingredients into a 1-gallon resealable plastic bag:

- 4 scoops of vanilla ice cream or vanilla yogurt
- 4 teaspoons frozen limeade concentrate
- 1 banana, peeled and chopped into small chunks
- ⅓ cup milk (omit if using yogurt)

Squeeze the air out of the bag, and seal. Gently squish the ingredients until mixed. Clip a corner of the bag, and squish the smoothie into four small cups.

To serve, place the smoothies on the Serve and Share Platter. Serve to your friends and family.

As you enjoy your smoothie, discuss this question:

- **What has God given to you that you can share with others?**

Read Luke 12:16-21 together.

# Parable of the Great Banquet

## PARABLE POINT Say "Yes" to Jesus
### Luke 14:15-24

In this lesson preschoolers will learn to say "yes" to Jesus as they explore the parable of the great banquet.

• • • • • • • • • • • • • • • • • • • • • • • • • • • • • • • • • • • • •

## A Message From Mary

I have an invitation for you. Would you like to go to a party? (Did you say "party"?) If you were invited to the best party of all—one that promised to give you eternal life—would you stay home? Would you be too busy for the King of kings?

Well, that's the kind of invitation God has given us through his son, Jesus. This great banquet is the party of all parties. Are we going to "think about it"...or are we going to say "yes" to the host?

As we invite our children to participate in these sessions, we are encouraging them to say yes to the greatest Host. Thanks so much to you for saying yes to Jesus. Once again, God bless you for the hugs you give them, the love you share, and most of all, for saying yes to God's invitation.

• • • • • • • • • • • • • • • • • • • • • • • • • • • • • • • • •

## Supply List

- ❑ CD player
- ❑ *Simple Stories Jesus Told* CD (track 9)
- ❑ Bible
- ❑ crayons
- ❑ large sheets of white paper
- ❑ party hats

- ❑ festive napkins
- ❑ festive cups
- ❑ graham crackers
- ❑ lemonade
- ❑ masking tape
- ❑ 2 cell phones (optional)

# Welcoming Activity:
## Getting Ready for the Banquet

• • • • • • • • • • • • • • • • • • • • • • • • • • • • • • • • • • •

Before children arrive, set out crayons and a large piece of white paper for each child.

After you've warmly greeted preschoolers, say: **I'm going to have a banquet today! A banquet is a party where people eat. A party like this needs fancy placemats. We're going to make placemats for the banquet. You can make a placemat by decorating your paper with the crayons.**

As kids work, go up to each individual child and ask: [Child's name], **will you come to my banquet this morning?**

When children have finished their placemats, clear away the materials and say: **What beautiful placemats you've made! We'll have the banquet later this morning. Our banquet will be like a party.** Ask:

• **Have you ever invited friends over for a party?**

• **How would you feel if none of your friends came to your party?**

Let children answer and then say: **I'm so glad that each of you will be at my banquet today. It makes me happy that you want to be with me, because I like to be with you!**

**Jesus wants to be with you too. He told a parable about how he wants to be with you. A parable is a story that teaches us about God. Today our parable is about a king who gave a banquet. God is like a king inviting us to _his_ banquet.**

**A king has tasty food to give to his people. And it's nice to be with the king because the king loves his people so much.**

**I'd like to tell you the story Jesus told—and I need you to help me!**

## For Extra Fun!

• • • • • • • • • • • • • • • •

If you have access to two cell phones, leave the room with one of them, then call an adult helper in the room. Have the helper pass the phone from one child to another as you say: [Child's name], **this is** [your name]. **Will you come to my banquet today?** Preschoolers will love this chance to talk on the phone!

• • • • • • • • • • • • • • • •

# Parable Discovery:
## Parable of the Great Banquet

• • • • • • • • • • • • • • • • • • • • • • • • • • • • • • • • • • •

Sit in a chair and gather children in front of you. Show children your open Bible. Say: **Jesus first told this story, and it's in our Bibles in the book of Luke. As I tell you the story, you can help me by acting it out. Let's get started.**

**Once there was a man who lived in a great big house.** _(Stretch your arms out to the sides as you say "great big house.")_ **Let's open our arms wide for the great big house.**

The man decided to give a banquet. He invited many guests. When the food was ready, he sent his servant to say to everyone *(cupping your hands around your mouth),* "**Come, for everything is now ready.**" *(Have kids cup their hands around their mouths and repeat after you, "Come, for everything is now ready.")*

But all of the people made excuses not to come! One man said, "I just bought a field, and I need to go look at it." That wasn't good! *(Shake your head "no" and wag your finger. Lead the children in this motion as well.)*

The second man said, "I have bought some animals, and I need to go see them." That wasn't good! *(Shake your head "no" and wag your finger. Lead the children in this motion as well.)*

Another person said, "I just got married. I can't come." That wasn't good! *(Shake your head "no" and wag your finger. Lead the children in this motion as well.)*

The servant went back to the big house and told his master. The master was mad! What face do you make when you're mad? *(Have the kids show you their mad faces.)*

The master told the servant, "Go invite the poor people in the town, and the ones who are blind or sick or can't walk." The master knew that they would say yes to his banquet! They would get to eat the good food. Yum! *(Rub your stomach and have kids do the same.)*

The servant said, "Even with all those people, there will still be room!"

The master said, "Then go outside of the town and invite even more people. Invite the people you see on the road. They will fill up my house." They would get to eat the good food too! *(Rub your stomach and have kids do the same.)*

It's too bad for the people who said no to the banquet. The master said that they wouldn't get a single taste! Let's make a sad face for those people.

Close your Bible and ask: **If the master invited you to his banquet, would you say yes?**

**PARABLE POINT**

Say: **Jesus wants for us to have a banquet with him one day. He wants for us to say yes! This story reminds us that we can say yes to Jesus.**

# Sing and Celebrate:
## "Wedding Feast" (track 9)

• • • • • • • • • • • • • • • • • • • • • • • • • • • • • • • • • • • •

Let children bounce and sway during this upbeat song. Have the kids follow you on these arm motions:

- When the lyrics tell how wonderful the feast will be, have kids rub their stomachs.
- When the song mentions guests who would not come, have kids shake their heads "no" and wag their fingers.
- When the lyrics invite guests to "Come to my wedding feast," have kids make "come along" gestures with their arms.

## "Wedding Feast"

I had a big wedding feast
With lots of goodies and lots of treats.
But my guests, they would not come.
Oh me, oh my, what can be done?
They all had an excuse or two,
Something more important they needed to do:
Wash the carriage, or socks to darn,
Or let the chickens out of the barn.

So come to my wedding feast.
I'll see ya there, so much to share.
Come to my wedding feast.
You gotta wear your best there.
Don't let time slip away from you,
With all the things that you gotta do.
Be prepared and ready to sing,
And dine with the King of kings.

So I sent out to the neighborhood,
Inviting everyone I could.
This wedding feast is fit for a king.
I told my neighbors to come and bring
The sick, the beggars, even the small.
They can sit with me at the ball.
Everyone's welcome, invite them all! Oh, yeah!

If you're not ready to dine with the King,
You'll miss out on so many things.
Come as you are, yeah, be prepared.
Know the one who invited you there.
Don't let time slip away from you,
With all the things that you gotta do.
Forget the carriage and socks to darn.
They'll let the chickens out of the barn.

Come to my wedding feast.

# Our Banquet

Let the children help set tables using the placemats they made and brightly colored cups and napkins. Help each child put on a party hat.

Serve graham crackers and lemonade. Tell kids how happy you are to have them at your banquet. Tell them you're glad they said "yes." Say: **My banquet is just a small one. Jesus invites you to a banquet even larger. At his banquet, there will be more to eat than graham crackers and lemonade.**

As kids eat, ask them about the parties they've had and been to. They'll enjoy sharing, and you'll get to know them better. Snack time is an ideal time to build relationships!

## Allergy Alert

Be aware that some children have food allergies that can be dangerous. Know your children, and consult with parents about allergies your kids may have. Also be sure to read food labels carefully as hidden ingredients can cause allergy problems.

# Bringing It Home

Give each child a piece of paper and crayons. For your own drawing, use a white board or a chalkboard, or tape your paper to the wall.

Say: **You're going to draw a picture by doing exactly what I do. You'll have to listen carefully to my instructions.** Lead the kids in drawing a large square, having them follow you one line at a time. Work slowly. Then lead kids in drawing a triangle on top of the square, as the roof for the house.

**By saying yes to my instructions, you drew a house. You said yes to me because you know that I care for you. Who cares for you at your house?** Kids can continue coloring as you all discuss.

Give children time to answer, then say: **Jesus gave you parents to care for you at home. When you do what they tell you to do, that's one way to say yes to Jesus. It makes Jesus happy when you say yes to their instructions.**

Let the children continue to draw and color their homes. As kids decorate their houses, suggest that they draw pictures of the people who care for them. Ask

## Teacher Tip

For younger children, you may want to prepare a connect-the-dot worksheet ahead of time. Draw four dots as the four corners of the square (the house). Make another dot above the square as the tip of the triangle (the roof). Kids then follow your instructions to draw from one dot to another.

questions about the people they draw, such as who they are and what sort of rules they give. Ask them why it's good to say yes to these instructions.

## Say "Yes" Hop

Using masking tape, make a starting line and a finish line about nine feet apart. Line kids up at the starting line, while you stand at the finish line.

Say: **I'm going to ask you some questions. Every time you answer yes, you can take one hop forward. If the answer is no, you have to stay where you are. After you've said yes enough times, you'll make it to me at the finish line.**

Ask questions such as:

- **Are we in Sunday school right now?**
- **Did you come here this morning in an airplane?**
- **Do you have green skin?**
- **Does Jesus love you?**
- **Do you love Jesus?**
- **Are you four years old?**
- **Are you five years old?**

Add questions as you like, and congratulate children as they reach the finish line. Play until each child has crossed the finish line. Give the children hugs and loudly cheer. Then say: **You made it to the finish line by saying yes. When you said no, you couldn't come any closer. Jesus wants you to say yes to him because he wants to be close to you. We can**  **say yes to Jesus.**

**PARABLE POINT**

## Together Prayer: Yes, Jesus

Say: **We can** say yes to Jesus when we pray. Let's get ready to pray right now. Let's put our hands together, bow our heads, and close our eyes so we won't be distracted by things around us.

**As we pray, I'll tell you things that Jesus said. You can agree by saying, "Yes, Jesus."**

Read the Scripture prayer below. As you read, encourage kids to respond with "Yes, Jesus."

Pray: **Jesus said, "Let little children come to me."**

**We say...Yes, Jesus.**

**Jesus said, "Follow me."**

**We say...Yes, Jesus.**

**Jesus said, "Come to me when you feel worried."**

**We say...Yes, Jesus.**

**Jesus said, "Learn from me."**

**We say...Yes, Jesus.**

**Jesus said, "Do you believe in me?"**

**We say...Yes, Jesus.**

**Jesus said, "Tell people about me."**

**We say...Yes, Jesus.**

**Jesus said, "I came to give my life for you."**

**Let's say, "Thank you, Jesus."**

**Thank you, Jesus.**

**Amen.**

# Parable of the Barren Fig Tree

**PARABLE POINT** God Is Patient With Us

Luke 13:6-9

What kind of fruit is on your tree? In the parable of the barren fig tree, preschoolers will discover that God patiently waits for us to "bear good fruit."

● ● ● ● ● ● ● ● ● ● ● ● ● ● ● ● ● ● ● ● ● ● ● ● ● ● ● ● ● ● ● ● ● ● ● ● ● ● ● ●

## A Message From Mary

I love to work in my garden. Sometimes, though, I get a little impatient when fruit trees won't produce anything. Sometimes it seems like forever for them to come around. I had a plum tree that quit bearing fruit, so we cut it down.

Aren't you glad that God keeps on waiting for us to grow? There's a reason Jesus used parables about tending the earth. They demonstrate how God creates growth in our lives. Just as our little ones are growing physically, you get to help them be fertile ground so God can help them grow spiritually and bear fruit. Like the song says, they're gonna grow!

I'm so glad you are patient with the children you serve. God will bless you as you share the great Savior's love with these little ones. Sometimes we receive even more from the love that we give. And as a result, you're gonna grow too!

*Mary Rice Hopkins*

● ● ● ● ● ● ● ● ● ● ● ● ● ● ● ● ● ● ● ● ● ● ● ● ● ● ● ● ● ● ● ● ● ● ● ● ● ● ● ●

## Supply List

❑ CD player
❑ *Simple Stories Jesus Told* CD (track 10)
❑ Bible
❑ 3 broken items
❑ elastic bandage
❑ lemon, apple, and orange
❑ photocopy of Rebus Pictures (p. 75)
❑ various kinds of chopped fruit
❑ paper plates
❑ disposable forks

❑ index cards
❑ crayons or markers
❑ craft sticks
❑ plastic foam cups
❑ potting soil
❑ seeds
❑ tape
❑ 4 large empty boxes
❑ beanbags, fake fruit, or foam balls

# Welcoming Activity:
## To Toss or Not to Toss?

Before children arrive, place three obviously broken items nearby. Wrap your arm or leg in an elastic bandage, but keep this hidden with long sleeves or pants.

Invite the children to sit on the floor in front of you. Say: **I'm so glad you're here today! I have some things I want you to look at with me.** Hold up the first broken item. **This is broken—really broken! What do you think I should do with it?** Give the children a minute to react. **You're right! I should probably throw it away. It is so broken it can never be fixed, and it isn't useful for anything.** Toss the item in the trash. If it is an item that could be recycled, set it aside and tell the children that you'll put it in the recycling bin later.

Hold up each of the last two items and talk about them, too. You may wish to have the children discuss what the items could have been used for. Finish by putting them in the trash too. Then say: **I have one more thing to show you. Reveal your bandaged arm or leg. What about people? What do we do with them when they're broken or not working quite right? Do we toss them in the trash?** Give the children plenty of time to react and discuss this. **Great ideas! You're right. People are precious, and we would never give up on them. God is the same way. Even if a person isn't working quite right or doing the things that he or she should,  God is patient with us, and he never gives up!**

**PARABLE POINT**

# Parable Discovery:
## Parable of the Barren Fig Tree

Before class make a photocopy of the Rebus Pictures found on page 75. You may wish to enlarge the pictures or even color them. You'll also need a lemon, an orange, and an apple close by.

Ask the children to sit on the floor in front of you. Open your Bible to Luke 13:6-9. Show the children your open Bible, and tell them that the story you're going to tell them comes from the Bible.

Hold up a lemon. Ask: **What is this? Good!** Hold up an apple. **What is this? Great!** Hold up an orange. **What is this? Super! If you saw these all together in a bowl, what would you call them? That's right. These are different kinds of fruit. Each of these grows on a different kind of tree.**

What if you had an apple tree that didn't grow any apples? Would it be very useful? Let the children discuss. Then say: **An apple tree without apples might give a little shade, but apple trees were meant to grow apples.**

Jesus told a short story about a tree that wasn't growing any fruit. This story is called the parable of the barren fig tree. *Barren* means the tree didn't grow any fruit, and a fig is a type of fruit.

I'd like you to help me tell the story. I have some pictures here. I'll hold up each picture and tell you what it is. When this character or thing comes up in the story, I'd like you to say its name out loud. Let's practice. Go through each one of the pictures, and then read the story to the children. When you come to a picture, point to or hold up the matching larger picture and have the children say that word out loud.

Jesus told this story called the parable of the barren fig [tree]. Once there was an [owner] of a vineyard. The [owner] had a fig [tree] planted in his vineyard. One day the [owner] went to look for [figs] on the [tree]. When the [owner] got to the [tree], he saw that there wasn't any [figs] on the [tree].

The [owner] went to the [caretaker] who took care of his vineyard. The [owner] said to the [caretaker], "For three years now I've been coming to look for [figs] on this fig [tree], and I haven't found any. Cut the [tree] down! Why should it use up the dirt?"

The [caretaker] said to the [owner], "Sir, leave the [tree] alone for one more year. I'll dig around the [tree] and fertilize it. If the [tree] grows [figs] next year, great! If the [tree] doesn't grow [figs], then let's cut it down!"

Jesus told this story to help us remember that God made each one of you special, and he wants you to grow good [figs] too! You can't grow this kind of [figs] (hold up the apple), but you can grow and learn to be loving, joyful, peaceful, patient, and kind.

Put aside the pictures and the fruit.

**PARABLE POINT**

Say: **When someone isn't being loving or kind, does God just throw that person away? Absolutely not! God is patient with us, and he helps us to grow.**

## Sing and Celebrate:
## "You're Gonna Grow" (track 10)

• • • • • • • • • • • • • • • • • • • • • • • • • • • •

Have the children stand in a circle and spread their arms as if they're the branches of trees. Explain that you're going to play the song "You're Gonna Grow" (track 10), and they can move like trees blowing in the breeze. During the chorus, have children squat down low to the ground and pretend to "grow" toward the ceiling.

## "You're Gonna Grow"

In my backyard, I've got a fig tree.

It doesn't bear any fruit or leaves.

Should I cut it down or let it grow?

My caretaker says, "Wait, and you'll know.

Give it care; give it time.

Wait a year, then you will find

What kind of fruit is on your tree."

What kind of love, do you see?

*(Chorus)*

You're gonna grow.

Grow.

*(Repeat)*

God says we're just like that tree.

But he waits patiently.

He says, "I wanna let you grow.

Show my love, and others will know.

Read my Word, and give you time.

By your love, they'll see that you're mine.

By the fruit that you bear.

What kind of love do you share?"

*(Repeat chorus.)*

The fruit of the Spirit is

Love and joy and peace and love.

The fruit of the Spirit is

Sent straight from above.

*(Repeat chorus.)*

# What Kind of Fruit?

Have the children clean their hands and then sit at a table. Give each child a plastic fork and a paper plate with a variety of chopped fruit to sample. As they snack, go to each child and ask the child to close his or her eyes. Select a piece of fruit for the child, and ask him or her to taste it and guess what it is without peeking. Let each child have a turn guessing a fruit by taste.

Go around the table and have each child tell about a time when he or she needed the "fruit" of patience—in line at a grocery store, when parents are busy, or when waiting for a turn with a toy, for example. Then ask when someone has had to be patient with them.

Encourage the children by saying: **In our story today, the farmer didn't just leave the fig tree alone for another year and expect it to grow fruit. No! Not only was he patient in giving the tree another chance, but he also did things to help the tree grow fruit! God is like that with us. Not only is he patient with us, but he also *helps* us learn to grow in good ways! He gives us patient and loving adults like parents and teachers to help us, and he gives us the Bible so that we can learn to grow good "fruit" too!**

## ! Allergy Alert

Be aware that some children have food allergies that can be dangerous. Know your children, and consult with parents about allergies your kids may have. Also be sure to read food labels carefully as hidden ingredients can cause allergy problems.

# My Patient Plant

Give each child an index card. Be sure each child's name is on his or her card. Set crayons on the table, and encourage each child to draw a picture of a plant on the card.

When their pictures are done, tape a craft stick to the back of each card. Help each child put a little dirt and a bean seed in a plastic foam cup. Add a small amount of water to moisten the dirt. Put the plant markers in to mark the plants.

Explain that these are "Patient Plants." Say: **It will take time for these seeds to sprout into plants. But be patient just like  God is patient with you! Your plant will need water and sunshine to make it grow. You need to take care of it like God takes care of you!**

**PARABLE POINT**

# Fruit Box Toss

Before children arrive, prepare four boxes. On one box write "love," and draw a heart; on the next write "joy," and trace a pair of hands spread out; on the third write "peace," and draw a star; and on the fourth write "patience," and draw a smiley face.

Put the boxes close together in a line. Have the children sit in a line facing the boxes. Take turns throwing beanbags, fake fruit, or foam balls into the boxes. Have children try this sitting, standing, kneeling, or even with their eyes closed! As each ball lands in a box, have the rest of the children call out the name of the "fruit" on that box.

If you like, play "You're Gonna Grow" (track 10) while children play.

# Together Prayer: Fruity Prayer

Ask the children to stand in a circle. Hold a piece of fruit in your hand.

Say: **We're going to finish today with a Fruity Prayer! I'm going to start. I'll say thank you to God for being patient with me, and then I'll ask his help to grow a kind of fruit that people can grow like love, joy, peace, or patience. After I do, I'll pass this piece of fruit to the next person, and each of you can thank God and ask for help.**

**Dear God,**

**Thank you for being patient with me!**

**Please help me grow the fruit of _____.**

Repeat until each child has had a chance to pray. If a child feels uncomfortable praying in a group, encourage that child just to say, "Thank you, God," and pass the fruit to the next person.

**In Jesus' name we pray, amen.**

# Rebus Pictures

Farmer

Tree

Owner

Fruit

# Parable of the Two Houses

## PARABLE POINT Obey Jesus
### Matthew 7:24-29

In this lesson you'll lead your preschoolers through activities that explore the parable of the two houses to help children learn the importance of obeying Jesus.

## A Message From Mary

Would you live in a house that was sitting on top of a giant pile of Jell-o? Imagine what it would feel like during a storm!

My grandpa was a builder, my dad was a contractor, my brothers were builders, and I even married a contractor. I've learned that if we don't follow the plans and build a good foundation, the rest of the house may fall. In the same way, I know that I am much happier when I obey the road map that God has given me. After all, God is the architect of our lives, and nothing compares to the foundation we can build in Jesus.

Thank you for helping lay the right foundation in your children's lives. My good friends at Group Publishing and I want to assist you from the bottom up to build on God's principles. Thank you for helping lay the right foundation in your children's lives. You are a tool in his hands.

## Supply List

❑ CD player

❑ *Simple Stories Jesus Told* CD (track 11)

❑ Bible

❑ towel

❑ blocks

❑ sliced bread

❑ cheese slices

❑ disposable cups of water

❑ napkins

❑ paper plates

❑ hole punch

❑ yarn

❑ crayons

# Welcoming Activity: A Firm Foundation

Before children arrive, place a towel and some blocks on the floor. Encourage preschoolers to build with the blocks until everyone arrives. After you have greeted the children and gathered them around the towel, say: **I would like each of you to build a house with these blocks. Do you think it will be easy?** Let children respond. Encourage each child to take a turn building a simple house of blocks or stacking four blocks.

**Wow! You did a great job! But, I want to see if we can make it a little harder.** Have two helpers hold the towel about two feet above the ground. Have children attempt to build a house again, this time on the suspended towel. This task should be more difficult.

When all children have had a turn, ask: **Was it easier to build on the floor or on the towel?** Let children answer. Say: **Things always work best when we do them the right way. Today we're going to learn that rules help us do things the best way and that it's smart to follow those rules.**

## Teacher Tip

Remember to give those children holding the towel a turn building as well. Or have adult helpers hold the towel, and encourage them to gently shake the towel to create an unsteady foundation.

# Parable Discovery:
## Parable of the Two Houses

Sit in a chair and gather children in front of you. Open your Bible to Matthew, and lay it in your lap. Be sure children know the story you're sharing comes from God's Word. Use the following script to introduce and tell the parable of the two houses. Ask:

- **Do you have rules at your house?**
- **What's one rule your parents have made for your family?**
- **Why do parents make rules for us to follow?**

Affirm answers, then say: **Your parents make rules because they love you and want what's best for you. Do you know who else loves you and has rules to keep you safe? Jesus! Jesus loves you and wants you to follow God's rules in the Bible and to obey your parents. Do you know what it means to obey?** Affirm answers. **To obey means to follow the rules. It means to do what you are asked to do and not to do the things you know are wrong.**

**Today, I want to tell you a story that Jesus once told about two houses. This story is in our Bibles in the book of Matthew.** Draw attention to your open Bible. **Jesus used this story to show people how important it is to obey his rules. Will you help me tell this Bible story?** Assure children that everyone can help. **Let me show you hand motions to some of the words in Jesus' story.**

Model and teach the following motions to the children:

**House:** Place index fingers and thumbs together at eye level to create a triangle or the roof of a house.

**Rock:** Firmly place one fist in the other palm, making a clap sound.

**Sand:** Hold hands palm down with thumbs touching each other. Move hands apart as if sand is separating.

**Rain:** Wiggle fingers up and down as if raindrops are falling.

**Wind:** Gently wave hands back and forth.

Say: **Are you ready to help me? Stand up.**

Each time you come to an emphasized word, do the corresponding motion, and encourage children to join in.

**Jesus said that people who hear his rules and obey are like a smart man who built his *house* on a *rock*. Let's build a sturdy *house*.** Make fists and pound them one on top of the other, as if building. **The *rain* came and the *wind* blew, but the *house* did not fall because it was built on the *rock*.**

**Then Jesus said that people who hear his rules and do not obey are like a silly man who built his *house* on sand. Let's build this man a sturdy *house* too.** Make fists and pound them one on top of the other, as if building. **The *rain* came and the *wind* blew. Oh no! The *house* fell down with a great big crash!** Have the children fall to the floor.

If you like, retell the story. Children will be able to anticipate the motions and learn the story better through repetition.

Say: **This story shows us how important it is to**  **obey Jesus. It is wise, or smart, to obey the rules Jesus has given us in the Bible. It's foolish not to obey Jesus, because his rules show us that he loves us and wants us to do things the best way.**

# Sing and Celebrate:
## "You Are the Rock" (track 11)

This song has a great beat and lends itself to creative movement. Have children stand in a circle so they can follow your motions and directions.

Before you play the song, have children squat down and make themselves as small as possible, creating a rock with their bodies. Say: **This song reminds us that it's smart to  obey Jesus.**

**PARABLE POINT**

During the chorus, have children squat into their rock shapes each time they hear the word *rock,* and stand with their hands on their hips when they hear the word *stand.* They may also wave their hands in the air as they sing *Jesus.* During the verse, let the children march in a circle.

Children may also enjoy using the motions used in the storytelling section.

## "You Are the Rock"

You are the rock

I stand upon.

You are the rock

I stand upon.

When the wind blows,

I know,

You are the rock—

Jesus.

The foolish man

Builds his house

On sinking sand (sinking sand).

But the wise man builds his house

On the rock that stands—

Jesus.

You are the rock (you are the rock)

I stand upon (I stand upon).

You are the rock (you are the rock)

I stand upon (I stand upon).

When the wind blows (when the wind blows),

I know (I know),

You are the rock (you are the rock)—

Jesus (Jesus).

The foolish man

Builds his house

On sinking sand (sinking sand).

But the wise man builds his house

On the rock that stands—

Jesus.

*(Breakdown)*

Rock, rock, build on the rock.

Jesus, you are the rock.

You are the rock. You are the rock—

Jesus, Jesus.

Rock!

# "Healthy House" Snack

Before passing out the snacks, cut half of the cheese slices in half diagonally, creating triangles. Cut the remaining slices in half horizontally, forming rectangles. Give each child a napkin, one slice of bread, one triangle of cheese, and one rectangle of cheese. Serve cups of cool water. Encourage children to place the rectangle on the bread as a door and the triangle above it as a roof, to create a house.

As children eat their snacks, sit with them and listen to the stories they share. Let them share about whom they obey at home, and what rules are hard or easy to obey at home.

 **Allergy Alert**

Be aware that some children have food allergies that can be dangerous. Know your children, and consult with parents about allergies your kids may have. Also be sure to read food labels carefully as hidden ingredients can cause allergy problems.

# "Obey Jesus" Wall Hanging

This wall hanging will provide preschoolers with a daily reminder to obey Jesus. Before class, print "I will obey Jesus" across the top of a paper plate for each child. Above the word *obey*, punch a hole and loop a six-inch length of yarn through the hole and tie a knot, creating a wall hanging.

**PARABLE POINT**

Say: **We're learning that we should ✿ obey Jesus, like the smart man in the Bible story.**

**PARABLE POINT**

**Today we're going to make something you can take home and hang up in your room that will remind you to ✿ obey Jesus and to follow his rules every day.**

**PARABLE POINT**

Give each child a prepared paper-plate wall hanging. Say: **Your paper plate says, "I will obey Jesus." Draw a picture of yourself with Jesus on your plate. When you see this hanging on your wall, you'll remember to ✿ obey Jesus.**

Provide crayons and let children begin. Sit with the children as they draw pictures of themselves. Write names on the plates of children who do not yet write. Talk with children about where they will hang their reminders to obey Jesus.

# I Can Obey

This game of simple commands lets children practice obeying Jesus.

Say: **Let's play a fun game that helps us practice obeying. I'll give a command, and you obey by doing the action.**

Give the following commands, and allow time for the children to obey. Younger children may benefit from you modeling the actions.

**Clap your hands.**

**Turn around.**

**Pat your head.**

**Jump up and down.**

**Hop on one foot.**

**Stomp your feet.**

**Touch your toes.**

**Shake your head.**

**Wave your arms.**

**Sit down.**

As you play, add actions as you like, and give the commands more quickly to make the game more active and fun. If you like, let one or more of the children have a turn being the leader who gives the commands for others to obey.

# Prayer to Obey

Gather children around you in a circle on the floor. Say: **Today we're learning to obey Jesus. We obey Jesus because his rules help keep us safe and because Jesus' rules show us that he loves us. Let's pray and thank God for all we have learned today.**

Have children bow their heads and close their eyes. Say: **I'm going to start our prayer, then each person can take a turn. We'll ask God to help us obey, then name one rule we want help in obeying. For example, you might pray, "Help me to obey by picking up my toys when my dad asks me to."**

Begin the prayer, then allow children to each take a turn praying. If a child is uncomfortable praying out loud, just have that child say, "Help me obey," then move to the next child.

Pray: **Dear God, thank you for loving me. Please help me obey by** [name an activity]. **Amen.**

## For Extra Fun!

To add more challenge to craft time, have children lace yarn around their wall hangings. Punch holes about two inches apart all the way around the edges of the paper plates. Give each child a twenty-inch length of yarn with a piece of tape wrapped around one end to keep it from fraying. Starting with the hole above *obey*, children may lace the yarn through the holes around the plate. Remaining yarn becomes the loop to hang the plate.

# Parable of the Sower and the Seed

## PARABLE POINT Grow With Jesus

**Matthew 13:1-8**

In this lesson you'll help your preschoolers discover how they can grow with Jesus like the seeds that fell into fertile soil.

• • • • • • • • • • • • • • • • • • • • • • • • • • • • • • • • • • • • • • • • • • •

## A Message From Mary

Acorns just aren't very fulfilled. Life is only good when they grow in fertile soil and become oak trees. Do you think they lay on the ground, look up at the tree they fell from, and think, "I wanna grow up to be just like you?"

Our children look to role models too. You have the incredible fun of helping them see Jesus as what they want to grow up to be like. You get to help make their soil fertile.

Teaching these little ones this important principle and planting God's truth is the best job of all! I can't begin to thank you enough for hearing God's call as you teach. It is my prayer that these seeds that you plant will bear fruit for years to come. (And don't worry those old oak trees still get to "go nuts" every now and then.)

• • • • • • • • • • • • • • • • • • • • • • • • • • • • • • • • • • • • • • • • • • •

## Supply List

❑ CD player

❑ *Simple Stories Jesus Told* CD (track 12)

❑ Bible

❑ paper towels

❑ blocks

❑ snow cone cups or paper cups

❑ pillows

❑ white paper

❑ crayons

❑ heart stickers

❑ packaged fruit snacks

❑ disposable cups of juice

# Welcoming Activity: Watch Me Grow!

Greet children warmly as they enter the classroom. After everyone has arrived, ask: **How much have you grown since you were a baby?** Let kids show you how big they think they were when they were babies, and compare that to how big they are now.

**Let's pretend we're babies. What would a baby do?** Let children crawl, pretend to cry, and so on. **Now let's grow back into preschoolers.** Have children stop pretending to be babies.

**Let's pretend we're baby plants in the ground.** With your preschoolers, squat very low on the floor. **Now let's see how tall we can grow!** Have kids pretend they are a growing plant by slowly standing up while reaching their hands in the air and then wiggling their fingers. **Today we are going to learn about a farmer who planted seeds and wanted them to grow like you just did. We'll find out what happened to the seeds he planted in different places, and we'll learn that we can 🌱 grow with Jesus.**

# Parable Discovery:
## Parable of the Sower and the Seed

Make a short path of paper towels. Nearby, spread some blocks for the rocky soil, paper cups turned upside down for thorns, and pillows for the good soil. Snow-cone cups are pointy, so they make ideal thorns; they're often available at larger stores such as Wal-Mart or Target. If they're not available in your area, you can use paper cups.

Have preschoolers sit on the floor as you tell the story. Open your Bible to Matthew 13, and show children that the story you're going to share comes from God's Word.

Say: **Today I'm going to tell you a story about a farmer who was planting seeds.** Stand and make spreading motions as you talk, as if you're the farmer. **The farmer tossed seeds from his pouch as he walked. The seeds fell all over the place! Some of the farmer's seeds fell on the path.** Have a few of the children squat down on the paper towels as if they're seeds. **Then**

**birds came and carried those seeds away.** Have other children pretend to be birds and fly to the "seeds" on the paper towels and gently move them off the paper towels.

**Other seeds fell on some rocks.** Point to the blocks. **When the sun came out, it was too hot and the plants withered.** Pretend to wither to the ground and have kids do the same.

**Other seeds the farmer tossed fell into some thorns.** Have children gather around the upside-down cups, hold hands with you, and start to stand up, then fall gently back to the floor. **The thorns choked the plants so they couldn't grow, just like we couldn't stand up.**

**Some of the farmer's seeds fell on good soil.** Lead kids to the pillows, and have them sit. **In this soil, the farmer's seeds were able to grow up tall and strong!** Have kids stand up and reach up as high as they can. **God**

**PARABLE POINT**  **wants us to grow tall and strong, just like the farmer's plants did. When we have love in our hearts and obey God, we can**  **grow with Jesus.**

# Sing and Celebrate:
## "Grow Me Up Like You" (track 12)

**PARABLE POINT**      Say: **We're going to listen to a song that teaches us what God wants us to have in our hearts and to obey God so we can**  **grow with Jesus.**

Let children act out the farmer's actions, spreading seeds, during the first verse. When the lyrics talk about growing, have kids squat and grow as if they're plants.

When the song mentions planting God's Word of love in our hearts, have children place their hands over their hearts.


## "Grow Me Up Like You"

Grow me up.

Grow me up now.


The farmer planted his seeds.

He put them in a row.

But some fell on the rocky soil.

They didn't want to grow. (No!)

But soon the seeds they fell again

Upon the fertile ground,

And the roots went deep from the care he gave.

They bear fruit all around.

*(Chorus)*

Grow me up like you,

Lord, in all I do.

Plant your Word within my heart.

Plant God's Word within my heart.

Plant your Word within my heart.

Grow me up like you.

The fruit of the Spirit comes

When we grow like him.

Love and peace and joy

And kindness never end.

I'll plant the seeds of love,

So everyone can see

The Savior's love has come

To live in you and me.

*(Repeat chorus twice.)*

Grow me up like you.

## Fruity Favorites

Serve packaged fruit snacks and cups of juice. As children eat snacks, talk about how to grow love in our hearts. Encourage children to share about who loves them, who they love, how they can show love, and ways to be kind to one another. Be sure not to force any children who aren't comfortable sharing, but encourage them to share their thoughts.

 **Allergy Alert**

Be aware that some children have food allergies that can be dangerous. Know your children, and consult with parents about allergies your kids may have. Also be sure to read food labels carefully as hidden ingredients can cause allergy problems.

## Growing Hearts

Give each child a sheet of paper, and make the crayons and heart-shaped stickers available.

Say: **God wants us to have love in our hearts and to obey him so that we can grow with Jesus.**

**Let's draw growing plants, but instead of flowers or fruit on our plants, let's let them grow hearts of love.**

**PARABLE POINT**

Demonstrate how to draw a plant such as a tree, corn stalk, or flower, but instead of flowers or fruit, let children use the heart stickers.

As children work, remind them that the hearts represent God's love and the love God wants to grow in our hearts. Talk about ways children can show love.

**For Extra Fun!**

Play "Grow Me Up Like You" (track 12) while children work on their pictures.

When children have finished their pictures, gather together and let each child show his or her artwork. See if children can name a different way to show love for each heart on their pictures.

## Hear and Obey

In this simple game, children will learn that in order to know what God wants them to do to help them grow, they must listen.

Have kids stand in front of you. Say: **I'm going to call your name. When you hear me call your name, I want you to come stand by me.** Have kids place their hands over their ears, and then quietly call their names. After you've called several names, have kids remove their hands from their ears. **It was really hard to hear me with your ears covered, wasn't it? Now I'm going to call your names again, and this time I'm sure you'll be able to hear me.** Call each child over to you by name. Have children form a circle around you.

**Now I'm going to tell all of you to do something, but you'll have to be quiet and listen carefully.**

Softly whisper instructions to children, either individually or as a group. You might instruct a child to give someone a hug, tell all the children to turn around in a circle, ask kids to give high fives, and so on.

Say: **God wants us to listen to him with our ears open and not covered up. That way we can hear what he wants to tell us, and we can have his love in our hearts and obey him so that we can grow with Jesus.**

**PARABLE POINT**

# Together Prayer: Listen and Grow

Say: **God loves us so much, and he tells us how we can grow up the way he wants—with love in our hearts.**

**Let's take time now to pray and thank God for telling us how to grow with Jesus and ask him to help us listen to him.**

Encourage your preschoolers to pray, but don't force them to if they don't want to. Show your preschoolers love as they leave by smiling at them and giving gentle hugs.

# Parable of the Unmerciful Servant

## PARABLE POINT Forgive Others

### Matthew 18:21-35

In this lesson you'll help your preschoolers learn that they need to be kind and forgive each other over and over again.

●●●●●●●●●●●●●●●●●●●●●●●●●●●●●●●●●●●●●●●●●●●●●●●●

## A Message From Mary

Why is it so hard to forgive? I don't know about you, but this story that Jesus told hits me more than any other. No matter how much we know we have to let go of our hurts and give them to God, it's difficult to move forward without forgiveness.

Jesus was the greatest example of loving and forgiving. He died to provide a way for forgiveness of my sins and yours, even though he was sinless and didn't deserve it.

In this parable, the master forgave the debt of the servant and expected the servant to do the same for others. In the same way, we are here to demonstrate to our children that forgiving our brother or sister for something that seems unforgivable is our way of thanking God for forgiving us.

The word "forgive" has many meanings to all of us. At the core is the word "give."

God bless all you do to give of yourself, over and over again.

●●●●●●●●●●●●●●●●●●●●●●●●●●●●●●    ●●●●●●●●●●●●●●●

## Supply List

❑ CD player
❑ *Simple Stories Jesus Told* CD (track 13)
❑ Bible
❑ clean sand
❑ disposable cups
❑ star stickers
❑ 2 undecorated star-shaped cookies per child
❑ paper plates
❑ white or yellow frosting

❑ candy sprinkles
❑ craft sticks
❑ disposable cups of water
❑ paper
❑ crayons
❑ heart stickers
❑ glue sticks
❑ glitter

# Welcoming Activity:
## More Than the Stars and the Sand

• • • • • • • • • • • • • • • • • • • • • • • • • • • • • • • • • • • • • •

Greet children with a warm smile as they enter the classroom. Be sure to speak the names of your preschoolers, which will make children feel especially welcomed. Ask:

- **Has anyone ever done something mean to you and then later said he or she was sorry?**
- **What do you think Jesus would want you to do?**

Say: **Jesus would want us to forgive that person. Today, we're going to learn what it means to forgive, and we'll find out how many times Jesus tells us we need to forgive others. Jesus forgives us more times than there are stars in the sky and more than there is sand on the ground. How many stars do you think there are in the sky?** Let your preschoolers give you their guesses, and then say: **Scientists that study the stars can't really say how many there are, but some say there are billions and billions of them—more than we're able to count!**

**How much sand do you think there is on the earth? I don't think any person has ever even counted that high! Let's take a look at just a little bit of sand and see if we can count how many grains there are.**

Give each child a cup with about a teaspoon of clean sand in it. Say: **Let's try to count the grains of sand in our cups.** Give children a little bit of time to try counting the grains of sand in their cups. Remember that most preschoolers can't count very high, so don't wait too long to continue. After a few moments, ask: **Has anyone finished counting all the sand yet?** Then say: **Wow! I don't think I can count all of this sand. And this is just a small part of all the sand in the world! Isn't it amazing to think about how many times Jesus forgives us? Let's look at the Bible to find out what Jesus tells us about forgiving others.**

# Parable Discovery:
## Parable of the Unmerciful Servant

• • • • • • • • • • • • • • • • • • • • • • • • • • • • • • • • • • • • • •

Open your Bible to Matthew 18, and show children that the story you're going to share comes from the Bible.

Say: **One time Jesus was talking to his friend Peter, and Peter asked Jesus**

**PARABLE POINT**

## Teacher Tip
• • • • • • • • • • • •

Be sure that you bring in *clean* sand for kids to use. You may want to consider doing the sand counting outside, where it won't matter if sand gets spilled.

• • • • • • • • • • • •

## For Extra Fun!
• • • • • • • • • • • •

Bring in an astronomy poster that shows stars. Have preschoolers try to count all of the stars on the poster when you ask them how many stars they think are in the sky.

• • • • • • • • • • • •

how many times he should forgive someone who had hurt him. Jesus told Peter a story to help Peter understand that we should always  forgive others. We can read this story in the Bible.

**Our story is about a king who was very kind to his servant. That's called** *showing mercy.* **Let's look at our Bible story and find out what happened.**

Have kids form two groups. One group will be Kings; the other group will be Servants. Have the Kings sit on chairs, and have the Servants stand in front of the Kings.

Say: **There was a man who worked for a king. He owed the king a lot of money and couldn't pay him. One day the man had to go to the king to talk about the money he owed. The man couldn't pay back the money he owed, so the king was going to sell the man and his family so he could get his money. The man begged the king to be kind to him and let him pay him back. He asked the king to please not sell him and his family.**

Have the Servants kneel on the floor as if they are asking for mercy.

Say: **The king was very kind to the man and told him he didn't have to pay the money back, and that he wouldn't sell his family.**

Have the Kings put their hands on the shoulders of the Servants to demonstrate showing kindness.

**The man was very happy!** Have the Servants jump up and down, then have the Servants hug the Kings.

**Now there was another man who owed money to the servant.** Have the kids who are the Kings trade places with the kids who are the Servants.

**The servant wasn't like the king. He wasn't at all nice to the man who owed him money. Instead of forgiving him, he made him go to jail.** Have kids turn around so that they are standing back to back.

**The king had been so kind to the servant that owed him money, but when that man had a chance to also be kind, he wasn't kind at all!**

Have kids face you and sit on the floor. Ask:

• **Who do you think Jesus wants us to be more like, the king or the servant?**

• **What are ways we can be nice to each other?** Let your preschoolers share ways they can be kind to one another, such as sharing, hugging, or smiling at each other.

Say: **Another way to be kind is to  forgive others when they do things that aren't nice.**

## Sing and Celebrate: "Forgive" (track 13)

Say: **We're going to sing a song that reminds us of this Bible story and teaches us about forgiveness.**

Give each child several star stickers. They can put these on the backs of their hands or on their shirts. Explain that each time they hear the word *forgive* in the song, they should take one of their stars and put it on someone else.

Play the song, and help your preschoolers place the star stickers on each other as needed. When the song is over, children may keep any of the stickers they have left or discard them if the stickiness is gone.

## "Forgive"

Peter said, "Lord, how many times,
How many times must I forgive?"
Peter said, "Lord, how many times,
How many times must I forgive?"

*(Chorus)*
And Jesus said, "Oh, I forgive you
More than the stars and the sand."
And Jesus said, "Oh, I forgive you,
So you must forgive again."

It's like the servant who had a debt.

He couldn't repay what he owed or he spent,
So the master came, wiped it all clean.
But the servant couldn't forgive anything.

*(Repeat chorus.)*

So when someone hurts you,
Forgive the debt they owe,
For love doesn't keep counting.
Love's gonna let it go.

*(Repeat chorus.)*

## Star Treatment

Say: **For our snack today, we're going to decorate some special cookies. The song we sang reminded us to  forgive others as many times as there are stars in the sky! That's a lot of times, isn't it? We're going to decorate star cookies, but we're not going to eat them yet. We'll do something else special with them when we're done. So don't eat them when you're done decorating.**

Help children clean their hands. Give each child two undecorated star-shaped cookies on a paper plate. Help each preschooler use a craft stick to spread frosting on two cookies and decorate them with sprinkles. After your preschoolers have finished decorating the cookies, have each child serve the cookies he or she decorated to two other preschoolers in the class. Make sure each child gets two cookies. Serve water, and let children enjoy the cookies!

Say: **Serving cookies to each other is a very kind thing to do. Forgiveness is another way to show kindness. Let's make something now that we can give to others to show forgiveness.**

## Allergy Alert

Be aware that some children have food allergies that can be dangerous. Know your children, and consult with parents about allergies your kids may have. Also be sure to read food labels carefully as hidden ingredients can cause allergy problems.

## "I Forgive You" Cards

Preschoolers will be making simple "I Forgive You" cards that they can give to others.

Say: **It is very important to say you're sorry when you do something wrong.** Ask: **Is it always easy to say you are sorry? Why not?** Allow children to answer. **What things do people have to say they're sorry for?** Again, allow children to answer.

Say: **When someone says that he or she is sorry, it is also very important that we say, "I forgive you." If we never forgave anyone, it would make people sad.** Ask: **What are ways we can show someone that we forgive him or her?** Allow preschoolers to respond. Some responses may be, "Say 'I forgive you,' " or "Give them a hug." Give children time to really think about how to show forgiveness, then say: **Today, we are going to make "I Forgive You" cards that you can give to show forgiveness to someone.**

Make paper and crayons available for the children to use. Have preschoolers show what their faces would look like if someone had forgiven them. Say: **Now I want you to draw a picture of the happiest face you can on your cards.**

After children have finished drawing the happy faces, give them heart stickers and star stickers to add to their cards. The hearts can remind them of the love they're showing when they forgive others; the stars can remind them to forgive others more times than they can count. Be sure each child's name is on his or her card.

Say: **Whenever you want to show someone forgiveness, you can give one of these cards and say, "I forgive you."**

# Forgiveness Tag

Gather preschoolers around you. Say: **We're going to play a game. When I say, "I forgive you, go forgive others," you'll go to others and say, "I forgive you." Each time you tell someone, "I forgive you," that person will run to someone else and say, "I forgive you." Keep doing this until you've told everyone in class, "I forgive you."**

Say to the first child, "I forgive you, go forgive others." Then let this child go and tell another child, "I forgive you." Then both children will go to others and say the same. Then the four children will go, and so on, until everyone has said, "I forgive you."

Say: **We're saying, "I forgive you," in this game, but Jesus wants us to forgive people even when we aren't playing a game. When friends say mean things or do things that might hurt us, like pulling hair or pushing us, Jesus wants us to forgive them. Let's pray now and ask the Lord to help us to  forgive others all the time.**

**PARABLE POINT**

# Together Prayer: Help Me Forgive

Say: **Jesus is a wonderful example to us for how many times we should forgive others. Jesus forgives us every time we ask him to. He wants us to do the same thing.**

**Let's take turns asking God to help us forgive others when they do things that hurt our feelings. You might pray something like, "Lord, help me to always  forgive others when they hurt my feelings."**

**Let's fold our hands, close our eyes, and take turns praying.**

**PARABLE POINT**

Give children each an opportunity to pray, encouraging them to do so. For those children who are hesitant to pray out loud, let them know that they can pray quietly to God and he will still hear them.

EVALUATION FOR
# Simple Stories Jesus Told

Please help Group Publishing, Inc., continue to provide innovative and useful resources for ministry. Please take a moment to fill out this evaluation and mail or fax it to us. Thanks!

*Group Publishing, Inc.*
*Attention: Product Development*
*P.O. Box 481*
*Loveland, CO 80539*
*Fax: (970) 292-4370*

1. As a whole, this book has been (circle one)
   *not very helpful*                                                                 *very helpful*
   1        2        3        4        5        6        7        8        9        10

2. The best things about this book:

3. Ways this book could be improved:

4. Things I will change because of this book:

5. Other books I'd like to see Group publish in the future:

6. Would you be interested in field-testing future Group products and giving us your feedback? If so, please fill in the information below:

Name _____

Church Name _____

Denomination _____ Church Size_____

Church Address _____

City_____ State _____ ZIP _____

Church Phone _____

E-mail _____

the 1 thing™

that everyone craves.

that really matters.

that gets undivided attention.

that can transform your life.

that encourages pastors.

that will re-energize you.

that will bring you joy.

that will unite your community.

that brings families closer.

that frees you.

that gives you focus.

that answers the why's.

that means true success.

that eliminates distractions.

that gives you real purpose.

that can transform your church.

Discover how *The 1 Thing* can revolutionize the way you approach ministry. It's engaging. Fun. Even shocking. But most of all, it's about re-thinking what "growing a relationship with Jesus" really means. Pick up Thom & Joani Schultz's inspiring new book today.